A PRAYER OF MOSES

A DEVOTIONAL STUDY OF PSALM 90

C.H. COBB

Published by Doorway Press
Greenville, OH, USA
doorwaypress.com

A Prayer of Moses: a devotional study of Psalm 90
Copyright 2013 C. H. Cobb
All rights reserved.

Find C. H. Cobb on the web at chcobb.com
or on Facebook as Chris Cobb. Signed copies are
available by ordering from chcobb.com. Print version
and Kindle versions are available on Amazon.com.
Contact the author for different E-versions.

ISBN-13: 978-0-9848875-2-1
Library of Congress Control Number: 2013945631
First Edition, 2013

Scripture quotations taken from the New American
Standard Bible®,
Copyright © 1960, 1962, 1963, 1968, 1971, 1972,
1973, 1975, 1977, 1995 by The Lockman Foundation
Used by permission. (www.Lockman.org)

Cover design by Dani Snell,
www.refractedlightreviews.com.
Cover photo is the copyrighted property of 123RF
Limited, their Contributors or Licensed Partners and is
being used with permission under license.

Dedication and Acknowledgments

To the Elders, Board, and congregation of Bible Fellowship Church, who generously provided me with a sabbatical and allowed Doris and I to remain in Greenville during the time without phone calls or interruptions. It was a *delight* to be able to worship each Sunday in my favorite church with my favorite people, and yet work unhindered on my studies. It's a great privilege to serve as the teaching pastor of this wonderful assembly! Thank you!

Robb and Scott, your sermon series through Philippians was rich, and was a great source of nourishment for me during my time out of the pulpit. Thank you for your work as brother elders and under-shepherds of the flock at BFC.

Robb, since the writing of this study, you've experienced the call of God into full-time missions. I know that you will be as great a blessing to MEDA, and the Seminary for Expository Preaching in Siguatepeque, Honduras, as you were to BFC during your ministry here.

Brent, John, Rich, Terry, Steve, David, and Carol, thank you for taking time out of your busy schedules to read and critique the manuscript. Most of your suggestions I have adopted. Any errors that remain are mine alone.

Soli Deo Gloria!

Contents

Introduction..3

Outline of Psalm 90..6

Translation of Psalm 90..8

Chapter 1: Thinking about . . . death......................................11

Chapter 2: Introducing Moses..21

Chapter 3: The Eternal Creator, vs 1-2....................................31

Chapter 4: The Wrathful Judge: Condemnation (Part 1), vs 3-6...41

Chapter 5: The Wrathful Judge: Condemnation (Part 2), v 7........51

Chapter 6: The Wrathful Judge: Sin (Part 1), vs 8-10...................63

Chapter 7: The Wrathful Judge: Sin (Part 2), v 11.......................75

Chapter 8: Our Response to God's Wrath, v 12..........................85

Chapter 9: A Plea for Covenant Compassion, v 13.......................93

Chapter 10: A Plea for Covenant Lovingkindness (Part 1), v 14.103

Chapter 11: A Plea for Covenant Lovingkindness (Part 2), v 15. 113

Chapter 12: A Plea for Covenant Fellowship, v 16......................125

Chapter 13: God the Gracious Sustainer, v 17............................135

Chapter 14: Jesus Christ, the Victor over Death!........................145

Appendix: Verse 3—An Announcement of Death or a Call to Repentance? Or Both?..153

Introduction

At some point—years ago—as a new Christian I encountered Psalm 90. While everything in the Bible was new and fresh, this poem stood out. At that time I was using the King James Version and verses 11 and 12 grabbed hold of my attention and have never turned loose: *Who knoweth the power of thine anger? even according to thy fear, so is thy wrath. So teach us to number our days, that we may apply our hearts unto wisdom.*

There was something there that had surpassing literary beauty and compelling spiritual power. It has stayed with me ever since. When the church of which I am the teaching pastor generously granted me a sabbatical in 2011, I spent the time reviewing Hebrew; my Hebrew skills had become very rusty since seminary (unfortunately, in the intervening months since my sabbatical my language skills have resumed their rusty condition —it's a fallen world). The review was intended to enable me to translate several psalms; I had five in mind. I got stuck in Psalm 90 and wound up spending the entire time chewing on Moses' prayer. It was time well spent.

Psalm 90 presents a balanced portrait of God as the Creator and Sustainer of life, the Wrathful Judge, and the Covenant Comforter. The Church today is comfortable with all of those vignettes except for the one concerning His wrath. We've lost an appreciation for God's terrible fiery judgment, as though it's something about which we should be embarrassed. Worse, some even deny that God expresses anger, as though it would render Him unworthy of our love.

The result of "sanitizing" God of His wrath is that we have diminished His holiness and righteousness. We've rendered God safe and the cross less necessary, or even unnecessary. In so doing we stand in danger of worshiping a god of our own making rather than the God revealed in Scripture. I believe that a careful study of Psalm 90 can go a long way toward restoring a proper appreciation of God's righteous wrath, which will bring us back to a high view of His blazing holiness. And along the way we will discover, to our unending joy, that everything in the psalm points us to Jesus Christ who delivers us from the wrath to come.

This study is intended for the church. Although I do brush up against academic issues at various points the layman is my intended audience. There are some important topics I have omitted. The earliest drafts of the manuscript contained references to the exilic audience of the psalm, in keeping with its placement at the head of Book IV in the Psalter. I have removed these references in the interests of brevity and simplicity. As a consequence, this treatment is lacking any consideration of the placement of Moses' prayer in the larger context of the book of Psalms.[1]

---

1 The arrangement of the Psalter is a matter of great interest and reveals something of the compositional history of the book. Psalms is divided into five

Psalm 90 is the prayer of Moses, the man of God. And Jesus is God's abundant answer to the prayer of His servant.

Let the words of my mouth and the meditation of my heart be acceptable in Thy sight, O LORD, my rock and my Redeemer. (Psalm 19:14)

"books." Psalm 1 begins Book I, Book II begins with Psalm 42, Psalm 73 marks the start of Book III, Psalm 90 stands at the head of Book IV, and Psalm 107 begins Book V. It is believed that Book IV was intended to minister to the exiles in Babylon in the sixth century BC, answering the many questions they had, such as "How long will our exile be? Have we been abandoned by God?" Even though Psalm 90 was written centuries before the exile, its placement at the head of Book IV gives an indication of how the ancient Jews understood its message.

Outline of Psalm 90[2]

1. God the Eternal Creator, 1-2
2. God the Wrathful Judge, 3-12
   A. The Origin of Judgment is the Fall, 3-7
      1) The condemnation is sovereignly enforced by God, 3
      2) The brevity of life is evidence, 4-6
      3) Divine wrath results in death, 7
   B. The Cause of Judgment is Sin, 8-11
      1) Our sins are comprehensively known to God, 8
      2) The brevity of life is evidence, 9-10
      3) Divine wrath is overpowering, 11
   C. Conclusion: In the light of coming judgment, help us live according to wisdom, 12
3. God the Covenant Comforter, 13-16
   A. A Plea for Covenant Compassion, 13
   B. A Plea for Covenant Lovingkindness to overpower the misery of chastening, 14-15

---

[2] Leupold's comment, "No one has yet found a theme that is big enough for this prayer" (H. C. Leupold, *Exposition of the Psalms* [1959; repr., Grand Rapids: Baker Book House, 1969], 642), should be kept in mind when examining this or any other outline for Psalm 90. I determined to focus on what the Psalm says about God, though many other useful approaches could be employed.

C. A Plea for Covenant Continuity, 16
4. God the Gracious Sustainer, 17
   A. A Plea for Grace, 17a
   B. A Plea for Permanence, 17b

Translation of Psalm 90[3]

1 A Prayer of Moses, the man of God.
Lord, you have been our dwelling place in all generations.

2 Before the mountains were born or you brought forth the land, or the world, even from everlasting to everlasting, you are *the* mighty God.

3 You cause man to return to dust, saying, "Return, sons of man!"[4]

4 For a thousand years in your eyes are as a day, like yesterday, because it has already passed, or as a watch division in the night.

5 You sweep them away and they die; in the morning they are as the green grass sprouting anew.

6 In the morning it flourishes and sprouts anew; at evening, it languishes and withers.

---

[3] This translation and the ones that appear at the head of each chapter, are mine. All other bible texts used in this study come from the *New American Standard Bible*, unless otherwise noted, and are used by permission. Where poetry is quoted at at the head of a session, it comes from the various verses of Isaac Watts' hymn, *O God our Help in Ages Past*, and is in the public domain.

[4] Literally, "sons of Adam."

7 For we have come to an end by your anger, and by your burning wrath we have been terrified.

8 You have set our iniquities before you, our secret sins in the light of your presence.

9 For all our days decline through your overflowing fury; we complete our years like a sigh.

10 The days of our life are seventy years, or if due to strength, eighty years, though their best is but trouble and sorrow, for it passes quickly and we fly away.

11 Who knows the strength of your anger, or your overflowing fury according to the fear due you?

12 So teach us to number our days that we may gain a heart of wisdom.

13 Return, O Lord; how long? Have compassion on your servants!

14 Satisfy us in the morning with your lovingkindness, that we may cry out with joy and rejoice for all of our days.

15 Cause us to rejoice according to the days you have disciplined us; *according to the* years we have seen misery.

A Prayer of Moses

16 Let your work appear to your servants, and your splendor unto their sons.

17 May the delight of the Lord our God be upon us, and establish the work of our hands upon us, indeed, the work of our hands, establish it.

Chapter 1: Thinking about . . . death

Psalm 90 is about the frailty of life, a frailty whose consequence is certain death, and that long before we are ready for it. For example, verses 5-6 use the imagery of grass—here today, gone tomorrow—which leads Moses to the point of such frailty: "we have come to an end" (v. 7). At every opportunity the prophet directs our attention to the reality of our own approaching death.

Most of us don't readily think about this topic. It usually takes the death of someone close to us, or perhaps a brush with death personally for us to seriously contemplate that most final of all earthly events. But we should consider death while we are still able to change the manner in which we approach it. Moses says, in Psalm 90, *teach us to number our days, that we may gain a heart of wisdom*. Psalm 90 is going to meditate on the problem of death, so let's begin by thinking about our own encounters with mortality.

Though I have experienced the death of friends, church members, and more distant family members, I have had two particularly intimate experiences with death. My first was traumatic. Doris, my wife, was in her last trimester of pregnancy. We had already named the baby *Jessica Lea Cobb*; she was our third child. Jessica was born at home, prematurely, and we were both unprepared for this. Doris had been feeling poorly all morning, and then began to have contractions. We called the rescue squad and though they responded rapidly, it seemed they were forever in arriving. Doris was in

A PRAYER OF MOSES

labor and in pain; I was clueless and worried; we were both afraid. Just in time the paramedics arrived and delivered little Jessica.

My wife was placed in one ambulance, the baby in another, and off they roared to Hershey Medical Center in Hershey, Pennsylvania. Close friends stepped in to watch our children, Dani and Josh, then just five and three. I raced alone to the hospital not knowing what I would find. Hospitals are places where the forging of our character progresses far more rapidly and painfully than we would wish. I was not looking forward to the experience.

After I located Doris we began the long wait to learn what was going to happen to our little girl. At some point there was a miscommunication with the medical staff, or it could be that my hearing problems were beginning to manifest themselves. In any case, when the doctor came out to tell us of Jessica's status I thought I heard something to the effect that, "it's going to be a rough road but we think she will make it." I was relieved and began to hope; but it was not to be. Jessica died about ten hours later from a massive infection which was determined to have been the cause of her premature birth. All of our hopes and dreams and preparations for that little girl came to a screeching halt that fateful day. It leaves you . . . empty.

My heartbroken wife remained in the hospital that night under observation lest she, too, experience problems

CHAPTER 1: THINKING ABOUT . . . DEATH

from the infection. I stayed with her until late in the night. As I drove home alone my mind was gnawing on a question: *what in the world was God doing?*

The house had been in chaos when we all raced off to the hospital earlier in the day. I returned to a dark, empty home. I climbed the stairs wearily to my little study and discovered that our loving friends had already cleaned up the mess in the bedroom. Sitting at my desk I opened my Bible and began to read the psalms, looking for comfort. Somehow by the grace of God Psalm 119:68 spoke clearly to my heart. It was not what I was looking for but it was what God had prepared for me and it was satisfying. In the midst of my grief I found rest and contentment: *Thou art good and doest good; Teach me Thy statutes.*

I'd been to Bible college and was a careful student of the Word, but that night I learned the most profound theology at the feet of the psalmist: God is *good*, and what He does is *good*. I didn't know what He was doing but I rested in His goodness. It was enough to know that *He is good.*

My second intimate encounter with death was in February of 2011. My dad's health was rapidly failing; a defective heart valve began to threaten his life. He was at the point where we never knew if he would rally the next day or draw his last breath. Thankfully, he was alert until the very end. He knew that he was dying and had the blessed experience of saying his goodbyes to my mom, his beloved wife of 65 years, and to all of his children and grandchildren.

I had the privilege of being with him, mom, Josh, Dani, and my brother Lou the day before he died. Somehow I knew it was the last I would see him, and I wept briefly in my mother's arms. I have a treasured photo of Josh and Dani saying goodbye to grandpa (our youngest, Lauri, had been there several weeks earlier but was unable to return for this trip). We left and made the long drive back to Ohio.

There was a procedure that might help correct the damaged heart-valve and dad was scheduled to go for testing at UVA Medical Center early the next day. He never made the trip; he died in my brother's arms very early that morning. Dad's life was a life well-lived, a life lived to the fullest. He served his country as a fighter pilot in World War II, remaining in the Navy until he retired in 1966. He then went back to school and was trained to serve as an Episcopal priest, in which capacity he served until his retirement from that ministry in 1988. He was eighty-seven when he died.

Death is the ultimate abnormality; it is the clue that something is very, very wrong with this creation. Those who know the Bible understand that death is the result of sin. The first man, Adam, chose a path of rebellion against God, and all Adam's progeny have inherited the guilt of his sin as well as his evil, rebellious nature. Even little Jessica had a sinful nature from the time of

CHAPTER 1: THINKING ABOUT . . . DEATH

her conception, just like her daddy and mommy, and like her daddy's and mommy's parents, and their parents and so on.

Aging and death interrupts fruitful lives all too soon. The brevity and transitory nature of human life, the inevitability of death, and God's wrath against man's sin are among the major themes of Psalm 90, the prayer of Moses. Death is not something about which we are willing to think deeply. But we must learn to do so. Moses' prayer forces us to go down that path.

Why do we need to think about death? There may be many reasons, but the most important one is that when we begin to consider death, we begin to think about God Himself. For some of us it might be the only time we do. We need to learn of His wrath that we might be willing to hear of His mercy and flee to His Son. I hope that this study will encourage you to do just that.

A brief introduction to Psalm 90

We typically associate the psalms with David, and for good reason: no fewer then seventy-three of the psalms are ascribed to David's authorship in their captions.[1] However many are unaware that the great lawgiver, Moses, wrote more than the Pentateuch (Genesis-Deu-

---

[1] The psalm caption, or superscription, is the title that precedes the first verse and is normally set in a smaller font in an English bible. For example, if you turn to Psalm 90 you will see the caption, "A prayer of Moses, the man of God." There is on-going debate about whether or not the captions of the psalms should be considered part of the inspired text. In any case, it is part of the Hebrew Masoretic text and for our purposes I am considering it authoritative.

A PRAYER OF MOSES

teronomy); he also wrote a prayer that was included in the book of Psalms, specifically, Psalm 90.

Some scholars doubt that Moses himself wrote Psalm 90. In some cases they base their disagreement on the language and style of the psalm, others appeal to bits of the content (such as the claim that Moses could have hardly stated, as he did in verse one, that "all generations" have found God to be their dwelling place). None of the arguments I have seen are convincing. The content of the psalm argues (decisively, in my opinion) for actual Mosaic authorship. I agree with Delitzsch, who says: "There is scarcely any written memorial of antiquity which so brilliantly justifies the testimony of tradition concerning its origin as does this Psalm, ..."[2]

It is, perhaps, the earliest of any of the psalms. Leupold points out that this powerful psalm does not borrow from other psalms "or have any affinity with them."[3] If correct, that is a significant testimony of early (meaning, Mosaic) authorship. It also positions Moses as the human writer who brought to prominence the common biblical motif which represents the frailty of man as the grass of the field.[4] There are connections between this psalm and Moses' other writings: compare Psalm 90:1

---

[2] Franz Delitzsch, *Psalms*, vol. 5 of *Commentary on the Old Testament*, trans. James Martin (1867; repr., Grand Rapids: William B. Eerdmans Publishing Co., 1986), 3:48.

[3] H. C. Leupold, *Exposition of the Psalms* (1959; repr., Grand Rapids: Baker Book House, 1969), 641.

[4] Bildad the Shuhite in Job 8:11-13 is actually the first to use the metaphor equating man's life or deeds with a fragile plant. Evidently it must have been a common figure in early Hebrew culture.

with Deut. 33:27, Psalm 90:3 with Genesis 3:19, and Psalm 90:7-12 with Genesis 3 as a whole.

Of this majestic psalm Derek Kidner says, "Only Isaiah 40 can compare with this psalm for its presentation of God's grandeur and eternity over against the frailty of man. But while Isaiah is comforting, the psalm is chastened and sobering, even though the clouds disperse in the final prayer."[5]

MacLaren, cited by Leupold, says, "The sad and stately music of this great psalm befits the dirge of a world. How artificial and poor, beside its restrained emotion and majestic simplicity, do even the most deeply felt strains of other poets on the same theme sound! It preaches man's mortality in immortal words."[6]

Isaac Watts' great hymn, "O God Our Help in Ages Past" is a paraphrase of Psalm 90. It was written in the backdrop of the sufferings of the dissenting congregations at the hands of a human monarch, Queen Anne.[7] Watts' own father, a deacon in a dissenting congregation, was jailed for his religious views. The setting of the hymn is appropriate to this psalm, which laments God's righteous anger against sinful man. The text of the hymn is included in this commentary at appropriate

---

5 Derek Kidner, *Psalms 73-150*, vol. 16 of *Tyndale Old Testament Commentaries*, ed. Donald J. Wiseman (1975; repr., Downers Grove, IL: Inter-Varsity Press, 2008), 359.
6 Alexander MacLaren, *The Psalms*, in *The Expositors' Bible* (New York: Hodder and Stoughton, [no date]) (no page number), quoted in Leupold, 641.
7 The Dissenters were the congregations and individuals who separated from the state church, the Church of England.

places.

As to genre, Psalm 90 is characterized by Stuhlmueller as a "communal lament," although the absence of any statement about life after death and the lack of specific references to God's great historical deeds also gives the psalm an affinity to the wisdom literature.[8] VanGemeren divides the psalm into three parts (a "hymn of praise," 1-2; a "lament on the transience of life," 3-12; and a "prayer for the restoration of God's favor," 13-17), and indicates that a "wide variety of literary genres" are represented in that division.[9] Wilson finds "wisdom concerns" in the psalm.[10]

An encouraging theme that will emerge as we work our way through Psalm 90 is that *Jesus Christ is God's answer to Moses' impassioned prayer.* Though it may not appear so at first glance, our study will demonstrate that the psalm is decidedly Christ-centered.

Creative writing possessing great pathos, especially poetry, is forged in the crucible of the poet's own experience. We must enter the author's world if we hope to understand his words. If we would understand Psalm 90, then, we must review who Moses was and what he

---

8 Carroll Stuhlmueller, *Psalms*, in *Harper's Bible Commentary*, ed. James L. Mays (San Francisco: Harper & Row, and Society of Biblical Literature, 1988), 90:1(accessed in Logos).

9 Willem A. VanGemeren, *Psalm 90: Teach Us to Number Our Days* in *The Expositor's Bible Commentary, Volume 5, Revised Edition,* eds. Tremper Longman III and David E. Garland (Grand Rapids: Zondervan Publishing House, 2008), 689.

10 Gerald Wilson, *Psalms-Volume 1*, in *The NIV Application Commentary*, ed. Terry Muck (Grand Rapids: Zondervan, 2002), 74.

did. Acts 7:1-45 provides a succinct overview in Stephen's sermon to the Sanhedrin. The much longer account is found in the Old Testament books of Exodus through Deuteronomy. In the next chapter we will explore Moses' remarkable life as we gather information that will help us understand his prayer.

> *"Who understands the power of Thine anger, and Thy fury, according to the fear that is due Thee? So teach us to number our days, That we may present to Thee a heart of wisdom"*
> Psalm 90:11-12

Food for Thought

1. What have been your memorable encounters with death?

2. What thoughts or questions did your mind gnaw on following this experience?

3. What do you believe about death? Is it final, or is there conscious existence beyond it?

4. How does the reality of death influence the way you live your life?

5. Why might it be valuable to meditate on the brevity of life?

Chapter 2: Introducing Moses

Moses, the man of God

Moses was born in Egypt, probably circa 1525 BC[1]. The Hebrews were under cruel oppression from Pharaoh, to the point that the Egyptians were attempting to kill all the Hebrews' newborn boys (Exodus 1:15-16). Moses' mother, Jochebed (Exodus 6:20), managed to hide baby Moses for the first three months and then placed him in a water-proofed basket and put him into the Nile. Pharaoh's daughter found him, adopted him and hired Jochebed to nurse him not knowing that the woman was Moses' mother. The story is found in Exodus 2.

Moses was raised in Pharaoh's court as a favored son and received Egyptian training and education. Though the Bible does not elaborate on how this came to be, Moses apparently knew of his Hebrew heritage. Moses' life is divided neatly into three forty-year periods: up until age forty he lived in the palace as an Egyptian. About this time he observed an Egyptian overseer beating a Hebrew slave; Moses struck the Egyptian, killing him. As a consequence he had to flee Egypt (Exodus 2:11-15).

The next forty years were spent in the desert of Midi-

---

[1] The dating throughout this study is based upon the older, traditional dating which places the exodus in the mid-fifteenth century, circa 1445 BC. Though I am familiar with the argument for thirteenth-century dates, recent scholarship has suggested that the traditional dates are correct. In any case, any dates from this period of antiquity must be held rather loosely.

an.[2] During this time he gained a wife and children. At the conclusion of it he had the famous "burning bush" experience. God commissioned him to deliver the Hebrew nation from Egypt and to guide them into the Promised Land (Exodus 2:16-4:31) which He had long before promised to give to Abraham (see Genesis 12:1-3).

Moses traveled back to Egypt, and demanded from Pharaoh the release of the Hebrew nation so that they could worship their God. Pharaoh refused, saying, "Who is the LORD that I should obey His voice to let Israel go? I do not know the LORD, and besides, I will not let Israel go" (Exodus 5:1-2). Bad answer; one that Pharaoh would soon come to regret.

A series of ten plagues followed, all of which were designed to (a) glorify the God of Israel, (b) humiliate the gods of the Egyptians, and (c) convince Pharaoh to change his mind (Exodus 6-11). Pharaoh does not change his mind until God slays all the firstborn sons of Egypt, both man and beast (Exodus 12:29-36).[3]

---

[2] The location is uncertain, but is probably in northwest Arabia, on the east side of the Gulf of Aqaba.

[3] This final plague becomes the inauguration of the Jewish Passover. The death angel "passed over" (without inflicting death) all the houses where the proper sacrifices had been offered and whose doorposts had been marked with the blood of the sacrificial lamb (Exodus 12:1-28, 42-13:16). The Passover is later transformed at the Last Supper of Christ into the "Lord's supper" which we celebrate as communion. The relationship between the Passover and the Lord's Supper is not coincidental. The Lord's Supper is the celebration of the fulfillment of the final redemption provided by Jesus Christ of which the Passover was the promise and type.

Chapter 2: Introducing Moses

The Hebrew nation, the children of Israel, are then delivered from Egypt. When Pharaoh has a late-breaking change of heart and pursues them with his army, God miraculously leads His people through the Red Sea on dry ground. Pharaoh's army, trying to pass through in pursuit, are drowned (Exodus 13:17-14:31). It is after this event that we learn of Moses' skill as a poet: he writes a song celebrating Israel's deliverance and God's victory over Egypt. You can read Moses' song in Exodus 15:1-18.

One might think that Moses' trials were over now that Israel has safely escaped from Egypt. Not quite. Now God has to deliver *Moses* from the hands of an ungrateful Israelite nation. Immediately after the Red Sea event the people of God begin to grumble. The first complaint has to do with a lack of drinking water (Exodus 15:22-27).[4] Using Moses as His instrument God provides them with water. The next complaint deals with Israel's hunger for the food of Egypt; God gives them manna in response (Exodus 16). The people ignore and disobey God's instructions regarding collecting manna on the Sabbath and are rebuked by God (Exodus 16:22-30).

The sequence of grumbling and disobedience to God's commands and God's appointed leader Moses, followed by God's rebuke or judgment, becomes pervasive in Exodus, Leviticus and Numbers. Grasping this recurring pattern is critical for properly understanding

---

[4] Notice that the first complaint comes so quickly after their miraculous deliverance that it is recorded in the *same chapter* as Moses' victory song!

A PRAYER OF MOSES

Moses' references in Psalm 90 to man's sinfulness and God's wrath. Although examples abound, one of the more horrifying samples is found in Numbers 16 when some of the Levites, already a privileged class with respect to serving Israel's God, complain that they are not privileged enough! They accuse Moses of taking too much upon himself and they dishonor him. The account in the Bible conveys the horror of God's judgment upon these rebels:

> And Moses said, "By this you shall know that the LORD has sent me to do all these deeds; for this is not my doing. If these men die the death of all men, or if they suffer the fate of all men, then the LORD has not sent me. But if the LORD brings about an entirely new thing and the ground opens its mouth and swallows them up with all that is theirs, and they descend alive into Sheol, then you will understand that these men have spurned the LORD." Then it came about as he finished speaking all these words, that the ground that was under them split open; and the earth opened its mouth and swallowed them up, and their households, and all the men who belonged to Korah, with their possessions. So they and all that belonged to them went down alive to Sheol; and the earth closed over them, and they perished from the midst of the assembly. And all Israel who were around them fled at their outcry, for they said, "The earth

may swallow us up!" Fire also came forth from the LORD and consumed the two hundred and fifty men who were offering the incense. (Numbers 16:28-35)

Buried alive by the direct action of God's judgment! What a terrifying expression of God's righteous wrath and overflowing fury! But what happens next is mind-boggling: the people, having seen this horrific judgment, *blame Moses*! God's wrath is again kindled and by the time Moses and Aaron are able to make atonement 14,700 more people die (Numbers 16:41-50). These experiences doubtless contribute to the direction of Moses' thought in Psalm 90.

It is important that you and I, the readers of these texts, not make the mistake of seeing these people as cardboard-cutouts on a Sunday School bulletin board. These were living, breathing, bleeding, dying, grieving people; someone's aunt, uncle, mother, father, brother, sister, son, daughter! These were *actual* people who *actually* died in an *actual* judgment of God in response to their *actual* transgressions. In modern terms their names are on headstones in some graveyard somewhere, complete with their birth and death dates! If we miss this horrifying reality and allow these individuals to become sanitized cartoon characters we will fail to appropriately apply the psalm to our own very real lives. Most importantly, we will fail to fear God with the fear that is *due* Him (Psalm 90:11).

Moses' trials were not over. The nation had already refused to enter the Promised Land (Numbers 14), arrogantly accusing God of being incapable of protecting them and of having wicked motives.[5] The judgment arising from God's righteous anger at this new provocation was severe: forty years of wandering in the desert until the entire generation of unbelievers had died out,[6] a long, slow execution by "Father Time."[7] But in what must have been the most crushing blow of all Moses himself was condemned to die _outside_ of the Promised Land. At a crucial point in a moment of human fury he had disobeyed God's instructions and God punished even His special servant, Moses (Numbers 20:8-13).

Psalm 90, especially its perspectives of the brevity and sinfulness of human life and the overflowing fury of God's judgment, must be read in the light of Moses' own experiences. Even the fact that Psalm 90 is written as a *prayer* reaches back to a characteristic of Moses' own life. He was a great prayer warrior, constantly interceding on behalf of God's disobedient people.

---

[5] They charged God with the crime of bringing them into the desert *to kill them*, no less! If God desired to kill them He needed no desert to accomplish it. Interestingly, Psalm 90 does speak of God as the One who _causes_ death.

[6] This is the height of irony. God was ready to display His miraculous deliverance once again by bringing His people safely into the Promised Land. They, instead, accused Him of plotting to kill them (which is ludicrous on its face), leaving their helpless wives and children as plunder in the desert. So in judgment of their unbelief God *does* sentence them to death in the desert but promises He will bring their children, whom they said would be plunder, into the Land and give it to them. *Be it done to you according to your faith*, Matthew 9:29.

[7] This forty years comprises the final forty-year period of Moses' 120 year life.

When God was set to destroy the Israelites for their repeated rebellions, Moses would fall to his knees and cry out in their behalf. Psalm 90 stands as Moses' enduring intercession for the people of God. In one respect, Psalm 90 can be viewed as the John 17 of the Old Testament (see footnote 12).

Moses in the New Testament

Moses is presented in at least three important ways in the New Testament. First, he is referred to in his capacity as the lawgiver. As such, Moses' writing is used as the foundation of God's revealed law.[8] In debates and disputes in the New Testament Moses is referred to as the authoritative voice against which all other ideas must be measured and evaluated.[9] Second, Moses is <u>*compared*</u> with Jesus.[10] If Moses is believed, Christ will be believed. God would raise up a prophet like Moses (law-giver, deliverer, intercessor). Like Moses, Christ is faithful in all God asks of Him. Third, Moses is <u>*contrasted*</u> with Jesus.[11] One brings *Law*, the other, *Grace*. One promises that the keeper of the Law will *live* (but fails to keep the Law himself, as his own death witnesses), the other not only keeps the Law but also *grants life* to all those who express faith in Him. One is faithful as a *servant* in the Father's house, the other is faithful as the *Son* of the Father.

---

8 Moses wrote Genesis through Deuteronomy, a collection we call the "Pentateuch."
9 See for instance, Matt 8:4, 22:24, 23:1-3; Mark 10:2-3; Luke 24:27.
10 Not, however, as an equal. See for example, John 5:46, Acts 3:22; Hebrews 3:2.
11 See for example, John 1:17; Acts 13:39; Romans 10:4-13; Hebrews 3:3, 5-6.

A PRAYER OF MOSES

It is primarily in the light of Moses' *contrast* to Christ that Psalm 90 must be read.[12] In the end, Moses the great lawgiver is himself subject to God's wrath upon his own sins and dies short of the Promised Land. Moses, the deliverer of Israel, could not deliver himself from God's judgment. Psalm 90, the impassioned prayer Moses offers, will in fact be answered but only in the incomparable Person and saving work of Jesus Christ.

---

[12] However, Psalm 90 could be compared favorably with Jesus' High Priestly prayer of John 17, in that both prayers are intercessions for God's people prayed by God's chosen deliverers at or near the end of their earthly lives. But the differences are so vast (for example, Christ completed His work and obeyed all that the Father commanded, whereas Moses did not complete his work and died short of the Promised Land because of his own disobedience to the Father; one is a prayer of victory, the other is a plea for grace) that one could equally argue that John 17 is more of a contrast than a comparison. In any case, nowhere does the Scripture itself compare or contrast the two passages.

Food for Thought

1. What are three of the ways the New Testament speaks of Moses?

2. How was Moses qualified to be a witness of the wrath of God?

3. Read Psalm 90, and then list the more obvious themes with which it deals.

4. It appears there was no grace for Moses: one mistake and God's judgment fell upon him. What do you think is going on here?

5. Have you ever felt that you were the target of God's anger? How did you react?

Chapter 3: The Eternal Creator, vs 1-2

1 A Prayer of Moses, the man of God.
Lord, you have been our dwelling place in all generations.

> *O God, our help in ages past,*
> *Our hope for years to come,*
> *Our shelter from the stormy blast,*
> *And our eternal home.*
>
> *Under the shadow of Thy throne*
> *Still may we dwell secure;*
> *Sufficient is Thine arm alone,*
> *And our defense is sure.*[1]

A "**prayer**" psalm, or *tepillah* psalm, as identified by the caption, was a type of lament or entreaty for the writer himself or others for whom he was praying.[2] Moses was known for his intercessory prayers on behalf of God's people, particularly when they had sinned:

- When they had corrupted themselves with idols, and God was threatening to destroy them, Exodus 32:7-14, 30-35.

- When Aaron and Miriam complained against Moses' leadership, and God struck Miriam with leprosy, Numbers 12.

---
1 Isaac Watts, *O God Our Help in Ages Past*, vs 1, 2, http://en.wikipedia.org/wiki/O_God,_Our_Help_in_Ages_Past. (accessed July 12, 2011).
2 Wilson, 318-19. There are five *tepillah* psalms: 17, 86, 90, 102, and 142.

- When the nation refused to enter the land, and God threatened to destroy them, Numbers 14:11-25.

- When Korah, Dathan, and Abiram rebelled against Moses leadership, and God threatened to consume the congregation, Numbers 16:20-22.

- When the rebellion was resumed the next day, and God's wrath broke out among them, Numbers 16:41-50.

Other examples could be cited. The effectiveness of Moses' intercession is powerfully alluded to in Jeremiah 15:1: "Then the LORD said to me, 'Even though Moses and Samuel were to stand before Me, My heart would not be with this people; send them away from My presence and let them go!'" The idea is, "not *even* Moses would be able to pray them out of this fix!" Psalm 106:23 is a record of the impact of Moses' intercession for God's sinning people: "Therefore He said that He would destroy them, had not Moses His chosen one stood in the breach before Him, to turn away His wrath from destroying them." Psalm 90 is one of Moses' prayers, recorded and preserved for us by the Spirit of God.

The caption identifies him as "**the man of God**." When referencing God's faithful servants, this simple title is often preferred in the Old Testament to titles such as "prophet." A "man of God" is one who lives in obedi-

Chapter 3: The Eternal Creator, vs 1-2

ence to God.

God is addressed in this verse not as "Lord", but as "**Lord**", stressing his sovereign rule.[3] This identification is emphasized in verse 2 when He is identified not only as Creator, but as existing before all creation.

Whenever God's sovereignty appears adjacent to themes such as man's efficacy in prayer, or man's responsibility, we as humans begin scratching our heads and asking the question, "how are these two apparently irreconcilable things reconciled?" We may ask the question and explore the tension; but we may not demand an answer. Rather, we must humbly submit to these twin truths of Scripture and recognize that, at many points, our creaturely finitude is inadequate to comprehend the counsels of God.

VanGemeren notes that the metaphor of God as "**our dwelling place**" is related to the imagery of God's protection and that it is unsurprising that several manuscripts, along with the LXX, use the similar word "refuge" (Hebrew: *ma'oz*) instead of "dwelling place" (Hebrew: *ma'on*) at this point in the text.[4]

The relation between these two ideas is shown in Psalm

---

[3] The distinction can be seen in most English bibles by observing the difference in the typeset: one word appears in all capital letters, the other has only the initial letter capitalized. The former designates the use of *Yahweh* in the Hebrew text and is a name which stresses God as the Covenant Keeper; the latter designates the use of *'Adonai*, which emphasizes His mighty power and sovereign rule. Note that all transliterations in this work are given in non-academic, lexical forms, and not as the words appear in the text.

[4] VanGemeren, 690.

91: one for whom the Most High is a "dwelling place" (v 9), is one who "dwells in the shelter of the Most High" (v 1), to whom Yahweh is a "refuge" and a "fortress" and the object of faith (v 2). In Him is safety and security (vs 3-10). Those who make the Lord their dwelling place will find that He "answers" and "rescues" them (v 15), and shows them His "salvation" (v 16). "Psalms 90 and 91 take the concept of dwelling in the house of Yahweh and renew its hopeful expectation by speaking instead of making *Yahweh himself* the place of dwelling."[5]

Moses speaks of God as a dwelling place in his final blessing on the tribes: "The eternal God is a dwelling place, And underneath are the everlasting arms; And He drove out the enemy from before you, . . . " (Deuteronomy 33:27).

God, speaking through Ezekiel the prophet, uses the expression in connection with the blessings and security of the New Covenant:

> And I will make a covenant of peace with them; it will be an everlasting covenant with them. And I will place them and multiply them, and will set My sanctuary in their midst forever. My dwelling place also will be with them; and I will be their God, and they will be My people. And the nations will know that I am the LORD who

---

[5] Wilson, 910-911. Wilson points out that this "breaks out of the national, political, and geographical limitations of ancient Israel" (911). It prepares the way for the idea of "abiding in Christ."

CHAPTER 3: THE ETERNAL CREATOR, VS 1-2

> sanctifies Israel, when My sanctuary is in their midst forever. (Ezekiel 37:26-28)

While the New Testament speaks of believers corporately being built up as a temple of God, through which God dwells in us (Ephesians 2:22) such that *we* are *His* dwelling place, it also speaks of the converse: God as our dwelling place. This can be seen clearly in the notion of abiding in Christ, found in John 15:4-7. Abiding in Christ guarantees fruitfulness, something Moses seeks at the end of Psalm 90. Furthermore, Jesus Christ promises to those who abide in Him that their "fruit will remain" (John 15:16), which speaks directly to Moses' desire for the establishment of the works of his hands. This abiding brings great joy, of which Jesus speaks in John 15:11, and for which Moses prays in Psalm 90:14-15.

God has been a dwelling place for us **in all generations**. Evidently Moses is looking back to the patriarchs, beginning with Abraham. Alternatively, the meaning may be that every generation since Adam has had those whose faith rests in the Creator God.

Moses' confession here is not simply a statement about God with respect to man, but is preparing the way for the prophet's assertion of God's eternality in verse 2. Psalm 90 at its most fundamental level contrasts the eternal Creator, God, with the ephemeral creature, man. "This opening of the psalm corresponds to the close, in that God is seen here as *our* God, whose eternity is the answer, not simply the antithesis, to our homelessness and our brevity of life."[6]

2 Before the mountains were born or you brought forth the land, or the world, even from everlasting to everlasting, you are the mighty God.

> *Before the hills in order stood,*
> *Or earth received her frame,*
> *From everlasting Thou art God,*
> *To endless years the same.*[7]

Moses is staking out God's eternality, and asserting that God was God prior to creation. This establishes God's transcendence over creation; He is separate from the cosmos. Moses looks from eternity past to eternity future and finds God filling each view.

Of all that the prophet could have mentioned with respect to God's act of creation, he chooses the **mountains**, the **land**, and the **world**. In the blessing of Joseph (Genesis 49:26 and Deuteronomy 33:15) the hills are called, "everlasting." The everlasting hills, as part of God's work of creation, stand in firm contrast to man's own ephemeral life on the planet which is, as Moses is about to teach us in verses 5-6, of little more longevity than the grass of the field, which today is and tomorrow is cast into the furnace (Matthew 6:30).[8]

---

[6] Kidner, 359.
[7] Watts, v. 3.
[8] However, note well that the mighty God who created the "everlasting hills" also shatters them in judgment, Habakkuk 3:6. In the presence of His judgment nothing is able to stand before Him. See Revelation 6:14, 16:20, and 20:11.

Chapter 3: The Eternal Creator, vs 1-2

The terms for "land" and "world" are commonly found paired together in Scripture (twenty-five times, of which nine are in the psalms):[9]

- emphasizing the stable character of the cosmos: 1 Samuel 2:8; 1 Chronicles 16:30; Jeremiah 10:12, 51;15.

- emphasizing the authority that attaches to Yahweh as Creator of the Cosmos, Psalm 89:11, 33:8-9, 24:1, 90:2; Proverbs 8:26, 31.

- emphasizing Yahweh's role as judge: Job 34:13; Isaiah 26:9, 18, 34:1-7; Psalm 96:13, 98:9.

- emphasizing the fearful effects of God's visible approach to His creatures and creation: Nahum 1:5; 1 Chronicles 16:30; Psalm 77:18, 97:4.

Psalm 90 has an affinity with the first three of these emphases.

Moses uses the imagery of birth to describe creation. This does not mean that the writer borrowed the imagery from the creation epics of neighboring religions, as some have claimed, but rather that the use of birth imagery for creation describes God's eternal existence *prior* to any created thing in a manner particularly suited to poetry. The idea is that He had to exist prior to the cosmos in order to give birth to it.

His pre-existence also establishes His absolute sover-

---
[9] The list which follows is from Wilson, 447-448.

eignty over the entire cosmos, since He existed before it and brought it forth. Moses' God is not a local or tribal deity, but the God over all. The word the prophet employs here for "mighty God" (′el) is significant. VanGemeren indicates that the Canaanites (the inhabitants of the land when Israel arrived from Egypt) believed that El was the father of the gods, but that Baal, his son, had taken over his supremacy as ruler.[10] Moses' affirmation here is that no matter which direction you travel with respect to time, the God of the Hebrews *alone* is the mighty God and no one takes His place.

---

[10] VanGemeren, 690.

Food for Thought

Read Psalm 90, then focus on verses 1-2.

1. What does Moses mean when he calls God "our dwelling place?"

2. Think about your relationship with God. Loosely using the metaphor of "dwelling place," would you characterize God as the rich guy living on the high hill in the wealthy part of town, someone you rarely see? Or is He a neighbor, but maybe you've put up a high fence between His place and yours? Or is He the welcome Master, that sits at the head of your table? Why did you choose the answer you did?

3. Think about, "from everlasting to everlasting, you are the mighty God." What does it mean when we say that God is eternal?

4. God is the Creator. What are some implications of that fact for all humans?

Chapter 4: The Wrathful Judge: Condemnation (Part 1), vs 3-6

3 You cause man to return to dust, saying, "Return, sons of man!"[1]

Thy Word commands our flesh to dust,
Return, ye sons of men:
All nations rose from earth at first,
And turn to earth again.[2]

Moses here portrays God as a powerful sovereign whose spoken word is the sufficient agent to effect his will. God executes the penalty of death by commanding, "**Return, sons of man!**" The allusion is to Genesis 3:19: "By the sweat of your face You shall eat bread, Till you return to the ground, Because from it you were taken; For you are dust, And to dust you shall return." This brings to mind Genesis 5, which is little more than a running obituary of the generations of Adam's offspring and can be organized around the repeated phrase (eight occurrences), "and he died."

Because of God's condemnation of man's sin, the inexorable destiny of all humans is to **return to dust**, which is a metaphor for death.[3] The day of death is in

---
1 Literally, "sons of Adam".
2 Watts, original v. 4.
3 This is a very common OT metaphor for death; you can find it in Gen 3:19; Job 10:9; 17:16; 34:15; Ps 90:3; 104:29; Eccl 3:20, and elsewhere. However, in every case I have located, except for Ps. 90:3, the term for "dust" is *'aphar*, which is not employed here. Here it is *daka'*. See the appendix for a possible explanation for Moses' choice of terms.

A PRAYER OF MOSES

God's hands: we don't know *when* it will come, but we know with certainty that it *will* come. God, Who is our dwelling place throughout all generations, is also our judge. Mankind has been tried in His court, found guilty, and now awaits the sentence. The term translated "**man**" (*'enosh*) is one that emphasizes the creature's weakness and frailty, contrasting with the mighty sovereignty of the Creator in verses 1-2. Verses 5-10 further expose the fragility of man's life.

The experiences of Moses illustrate verse 3 and provide a clue as to what Moses was thinking when he penned these words. The most significant example is found in Numbers 14, when events in the desert came to an impasse. The spies Moses had sent to reconnoiter the Promised Land had returned and brought back a mixed report. The Promised Land had lived up to its billing: it was a lush, fruitful place. Unfortunately, it had already been claimed by others and the spies' report presented the inhabitants as unconquerable. Despite the confidence of Joshua and Caleb that God would fight for them, the children of Israel rebelled and refused to enter the land. The penalty for their rebellion was severe: they would wander the trackless wilderness for forty years, until everyone twenty years old and up died (excepting Joshua and Caleb). For the next forty years, then, Moses is leading a *condemned generation*:

> "Say to them, 'As I live,' says the LORD, 'just as you have spoken in My hearing, *so I will surely do to you; your corpses shall fall in this*

wilderness, even all your numbered men, according to your complete number from twenty years old and upward, who have grumbled against Me'" (Numbers 14:28-29, emphasis mine).

Moses had such a clear perspective of God's eternality contrasted with man's sin-caused mortality because he lived in the daily, dying reality of it. This is undoubtedly the proper interpretation of verse 3: the condemnation of Genesis 3, brought on by man's sin, yields death as a result; God *causes* men to return to dust.

And yet there is the hint of something more here. It appears possible that Moses *might* be employing a double entendre, in which verse 3 could also be understood as a call to repentence in view of the brevity of life and the coming wrath of God. If you are interested in exploring this idea further, be sure to read the appendix "**Verse 3—An Announcement of Death or a Call to Repentance? Or Both?**" If there is a double entendre, then both death and repentance leading to life can be read out of this short verse. At the very least, the ambiguity leads us to more thoughtful meditation. Perhaps that is what was intended.

4 For a thousand years in your eyes are as a day, like yesterday, because it has already passed, or as a watch division in the night.

A thousand ages in Thy sight

A PRAYER OF MOSES

> *Are like an evening gone;*
> *Short as the watch that ends the night*
> *Before the rising sun.*[4]

This verse leads off with a conjunction ("**for**" - *kiy*) which ties verses 4-6 together as a result of verse 3: our lives are oh-so-brief because God executes the judgment of death upon us as a result of our sin.[5]

God's perspective on time is laid out in this verse. One **thousand years** is no more than **a day** from God's vantage point. Not only like "a day" but "**like yesterday**" in that it has **already passed**. God lives in the eternal now. Moses has thus contrasted God's eternity with man's temporal perspective. For us one thousand years is a huge expanse of time, in which families, clans, and tribes flourish and then disappear, kingdoms rise and fall, and the geo-political face of the globe is altered numerous times. For God one thousand years is as trifling as a single four-hour **watch division in the night**, "through which a man may have slept normally without being aware of [its] passing."[6] "The changes of time are to Him no barrier restraining the realization of His counsel—a truth which has a terrible and a consolatory side. The poet dwells upon the fear which it pro-

---

4   Watts, original v. 5.
5   Leupold believes that the conjunction actually points back to verse 2 where Moses asserts the eternality of God (644). I agree with the contrast between man's ephemeral nature and God's eternality, but I believe the conjunction governs vs 4-6 and is pointing back to verse 3, expressing result.
6   Leupold, 644.

duces."[7]

Peter gives us his Spirit-inspired interpretation of Psalm 90:4 in 2 Peter 3:8. The apostle employs the "thousand years are as a day" theme to explain God's view of time, with particular application to the apparent delay of judgment and the Day of the Lord. Peter's explanation is that God is making room for repentance, and he exhorts his readers, "since all these things are to be destroyed, what sort of people ought you to be in holy conduct and godliness" (2 Peter 3:11). What Peter encourages his readers to consider, Moses asks from God Himself in Psalm 90:12 ("teach us to number our days. . . .").

The third chapter of 2 Peter has several affinities with the message of Psalm 90. We could paraphrase and condense both 2 Peter 3 and Psalm 90 into a single sentence, perhaps like this: *God lives forever, but our lives are very brief; therefore, in light of the coming death and judgment, use your time wisely!*

The reader should be careful here. Neither of these passages (Psalm 90:4; 2 Peter 3:8) provide a mathematical formula for interpreting time in Scripture (as in "one day equals one thousand years").[8] To imagine otherwise

---

7 Delitzsch, 3:52.
8 "Some Jews and Christians have attempted to map out the ages as a 'week' of thousand-year days because of this verse. But this is to overlook the last phrase, *or* (lit. 'and') *as a watch in the night*, which rules out any such woodenness of interpretation" (Kidner, 360). Religious history brims with the failed predictions of those who have attempted to employ verses such as Psalm 90:4 or 2 Peter 3:8 as some sort of interpretive key that will unlock the time of

A PRAYER OF MOSES

is to confuse the imagery of poetry with the precision of a math textbook. The intent is to contrast an interminably long period of time with a very short one, leading to the proper conclusion that God dwells outside of time and the fulfillment of His plans and promises of both blessing and judgment will come on a schedule unknown to us.

5 You sweep them away and they die; in the morning they are as the green grass sprouting anew.

6 In the morning it flourishes and sprouts anew; at evening, it languishes and withers.

> *The busy tribes of flesh and blood,*
> *With all their lives and cares,*
> *Are carried downwards by the flood,*
> *And lost in following years.*
>
> *Like flowery fields the nations stand*
> *Pleased with the morning light;*
> *The flowers beneath the mower's hand*
> *Lie withering ere 'tis night.*[9]

These two verses must be considered together. Moses begins by employing flood imagery with the verb "**sweep**" or "flood" (*zaram*). The same verb is used in one other place, Psalm 77:17 ("the clouds *poured out*

Christ's return. Entire cults (such as the Jehovah's Witnesses) have had their beginning enmeshed in such errors.

9 Watts, original vs. 6 and 8.

water"). The antecedent of **them** ("You sweep them away") is "men" in verse 3: those who are swept away and **die** (v 5) are the men whom God causes to return to dust (v 3).

The noun form of the verb "sweep", translated "storm" (*zerem*), provides some help with the image. Isaiah 28:2 pictures a judgment storm of the Lord: "Behold, the Lord has a strong and mighty agent; As a storm of hail, a tempest of destruction, Like a storm of mighty overflowing waters, He has cast it down to the earth with His hand."[10]

Moses employs the figure of being swept away and drowned by the rains of a mighty storm. The term, "they die" is literally "sleep," used metaphorically for the sleep of death.[11] Job 14:12 makes obvious the meaning of the metaphor: "So man lies down and does not rise. Until the heavens be no more, He will not awake nor be aroused out of his sleep."

The **morning** after the judgment flood, the **green grasses** are **sprouting anew**. But this is not a picture of victory after defeat or some sort of cycle of life. It would be a gross misinterpretation of the psalm to draw from it something of the persistence of life. It is rather a snapshot of frailty and brevity, for the grass flourishes

---
10 However, notice Isaiah 32:2: a coming King will provide a shelter from the storm! The images of Christ permeate the Old Testament!
11 RSV, ESV, and NLT translate it "dream". Literally it is "they are asleep". KJV, NIV, NET, and NASB render it as "sleep" or "sleep of death", in both cases as a metaphor for death. I have translated it with verbal force: "they die," which is the overall meaning of the expression.

in the morning only to **languish and wither** again in the **evening**.

This motif of grass as man's life is used repeatedly in Scripture and portrays the ephemeral character of man's life. The book of Job (which may be the first of the Old Testament books, chronologically, to use it) explicitly relates the temporary nature of water grasses (papyrus and bulrushes) to man's fragile existence (Bildad's speech, Job 8:8-18). Job, in his response to Zophar, uses a flower as a simile for the brevity of man's life (Job 14:1-2). The afflicted man of Psalm 102:11 complains that his days are a shadow, and that he withers like the grass. David in Psalm 103:15-18 uses the image as Moses does, contrasting man's frail and transitory life with God's everlasting faithfulness. Isaiah 40:6-8 does the same thing, only the contrast is with God's word which stands forever. In the New Testament James points to the rich man as one who will, like the grass, fade away (James 1:10-11). James' picture is virtually identical to the Old Testament image.

But with the words of Jesus an adjustment to the motif can be detected. In Matthew 6:30 (and Luke 12:28), Jesus actually distinguishes those of faith *from* the grass; while the grass will be burned, those of faith will be cared for by the Father. In similar manner, Peter (1 Peter 1:17-25) quotes Isaiah 40:6 but suggests that our new birth by the *imperishable seed* of the Word of God has changed our fortunes from that of the grass of the field to that of a permanent, enduring state of blessedness brought about by the resurrection of Christ. Surely this is the consummation towards which the motif points!

Moses has contrasted man's temporal nature with God's eternal sovereign control. God sweeps man away as easily as a flood carries off everything in its path. The judgment of death and the fleeting nature of life are even illustrated in Moses' leadership over Israel. As glorious and amazing as Moses' ministry was, it ultimately remained a "ministry of death" and a "ministry of condemnation" (2 Corinthians 3:7-9), not only from the perspective of the Egyptians, but *even from that of the covenant people*. It was not just those who directly rebelled against Moses who experienced death, but an entire *generation* died, wandering in the wilderness for forty years. Surely the experiences of Moses and Israel are reflected in these verses. "It was thoughts such as these that Moses and his generation, dying in the Wilderness of Paran, were led to consider. Life flees away; God endures."[12]

---

12 Leupold, 645.

Food for Thought

Read Psalm 90, then focus on verses 3-6.

1. Read Genesis 3. What does it mean to "turn man back into dust?

2. According to Genesis 3, Why does God turn man back into dust?

3. What does Moses mean in Psalm 90:4-6? What is he talking about?

4. When you have heard people talking about how short life seems, are they typically older people, or young people? Why is this?

5. The religious culture of our day disparages the fear of God, as though fearing Him is unnecessary. Since God has the power of life and death in His hands, how do you think we should respond to Him (see Luke 12:4-5)? What does that look like?

Chapter 5: The Wrathful Judge: Condemnation (Part 2), v 7

7 For we have come to an end by your anger, and by your burning wrath we have been terrified.

Once again the conjunction ("**for**", *kiy*) points back to verse 3, framing what follows as a result of God's condemnation of sin. After having painted a picture of man's transitory life using poetic images, Moses speaks very directly: it is because of the wrath of God we are consumed. Leupold's comments are to the point: "The profound cause of the brevity of mortal life is revealed. Two factors are intertwined. The final cause is man's sin. The operative cause is the wrath of God which is called forth by man's sin. Both these factors are stern realities."[1]

The verb "**come to an end**" is used by David in Psalm 39:10-11 in much the same way as here: "Remove Thy plague from me; Because of the opposition of Thy hand, *I am perishing*. With reproofs Thou dost chasten a man for iniquity; Thou dost consume as a moth what is precious to him; Surely every man is a mere breath" (emphasis mine).

Certainly in Moses' day Israel was coming to "an end;" an entire generation was dying under judgment and the wilderness was littered with their corpses. The wrath of God was a daily living, or shall we say, *dying* reality for the sinful children of Israel. Their pitiful cry recorded in Numbers 17:12-13 expresses a sense of doom: "Then

---
1 Leupold, 645.

the sons of Israel spoke to Moses, saying, 'Behold, we perish, we are dying, we are all dying! Everyone who comes near, who comes near to the tabernacle of the LORD, must die. Are we to perish completely?'" Isaiah 33:14 speaks of the same terror: "Sinners in Zion are terrified; Trembling has seized the godless. 'Who among us can live with the consuming fire? Who among us can live with continual burning?'" And even Moses himself will "**come to an end by your anger**" on the heights of Mount Nebo for his sin against God at Meribah (Numbers 20:12). Truly, as the writer of Hebrews says (quoting Moses, by the way), "our God is a consuming fire."[2]

Moses employs three terms in Psalm 90 to express God's righteous wrath:

- אַף (*'aph*)- translated in Psalm 90:7 as "anger." It expresses the emotional aspect of anger.[3] Its primary meaning refers the nose or face and it is translated that way several times in Scripture. When used to speak of anger it conjures a visual image of anger expressed in the face: a reddened

---

2 See Hebrews 12:29 and Deuteronomy 4:24.
3 Gerard Van Groningen, in R. Laird Harris, Gleason L. Archer, and Bruce K. Waltke, eds. *Theological Wordbook of the Old Testament*, 2 vols., (Chicago: Moody Press, 1980), 133a. (Cited in text as *TWOT*. All citations refer to article numbers, rather than volume and page numbers.) TWOT is an excellent resource, but can be improperly employed by the unwary. Words gain their meaning from their contexts. The wider the semantic range (range of meanings) of a word, the more important it is to allow the context to *narrow* its meaning. A word never carries its full semantic range into a particular context. Unless the author is using a double entendre, a word in a given context has only one meaning, regardless of the width of its possible range of meanings.

CHAPTER 5: THE WRATHFUL JUDGE: CONDEMNATION (PART 2), V 7

complexion, nostrils flaring, a fierce glare. Jeremiah 25:36-38 uses the term as he speaks of the Lord's anger, and its results:

> "Hear the sound of the cry of the shepherds, And the wailing of the masters of the flock! For the LORD is destroying their pasture, And the peaceful folds are made silent because of the fierce *anger* of the LORD. He has left His hiding place like the lion; For their land has become a horror because of the fierceness of the oppressing sword, And because of His fierce *anger*"(emphasis mine).

In Psalm 90:7, Moses gives us the poetic version of Romans 6:23, "the wages of sin is death," as he expresses that we come to an end or vanish (in the sense of perishing) through God's anger.

- חֵמָה (*chemah*) - translated in verse 7 as "**burning wrath**." The term belongs to a family of words all of which make reference to heat, or something hot. It is frequently used to refer to anger, rage, and fury. Psalm 37:8 uses it in parallel with *'aph*, clearly establishing at least the direction of its meaning: "Cease from anger [*'aph*], and forsake wrath [*chemah*]; Do not fret, it leads only to evildoing." Van Groningen points out that *chemah* sometimes refers to God's reaction to His covenant people when they are unfaithful.[4] Moses employs it that way: "For I was afraid of the anger [*'aph*] and hot displeasure [*chemah*] with which the LORD was wrathful against you in order to destroy you, but the LORD listened to me that time also" (Deuteronomy 9:19).

Van Groningen offers a significant theological observation: once God's wrath, *chemah,* has been kindled it is not satisfied apart from being poured out in the execution of judgment upon that which provoked it (see 2 Kings 22:13-17).[5] Sinners, then, are the target of God's judgment wrath. Hebrews tells us that not even the temple sacrifices could permanently atone for sin (Hebrews 10:4, 11). Christ alone is the sacrifice which permanently propitiates the Father's burning anger against sin (Hebrews 10:12-22). Instead of being poured upon us (as believers), God's wrath was poured out on the Son while He hung on the cross dying in our place (Isaiah 53). Unless hidden in Christ through faith in Him, the burning heat of God's anger will yet be expressed upon sinners themselves (John 3:36).

- עֶבְרָה (*'ebrah*)- This expression occurs in Psalm 90:9 and 11. The verbal root of this noun is *'abar*, to pass over, to overflow. Van Groningen indicates that "the ideas expressed by the

---
4 TWOT, 860a.
5 *Ibid.*

noun are a surpassing measure and/or excess."[6] Setting it apart from other terms for anger, "it adds the nuance of the fierceness of God's wrath (Ps 78:49) expressed in an overwhelming and complete demonstration (Isa 13:9). God's wrath burns, overflows, sweeps away everything before it (Ezk 22:21, 31)."[7] Psalm 78:49-50 looks *back* on God's deeds in history, especially the expression of God's wrath against Egypt leading to the deliverance of His covenant people:

> "He sent upon them His burning anger [’*aph*], fury [‘*ebrah*], and indignation, and trouble, a band of destroying angels. He leveled a path for His anger [’*aph*]; He did not spare their soul from death, But gave over their life to the plague. . . ."

Isaiah 13:9 looks *forward* to the day of the Lord, and has the same idea of God's anger sweeping away all before it: "Behold, the day of the LORD is coming, Cruel, with fury [‘*ebrah*] and burning anger [’*aph*], To make the land a desolation; And He will exterminate its sinners from it." As TWOT says, "Thus on the day of the Lord's [wrath], nothing stands before it."[8]

The display of God's anger produces sheer terror in man as he comes to his end. Moses was well-positioned

---
6 TWOT, 1556d.
7 *Ibid.*
8 *Ibid.*

to observe many horrific examples of God's wrath against sinners, and the theme permeates his prayer. It is God's wrath that has made life so short and fleeting. And yet as the next verse indicates, God's wrath is not arbitrary or capricious but the righteous measure of our rebellion against His sovereign authority.

The system of sacrifice that God gave to His people through Moses was designed to propitiate God's wrath. Since the wages of sin is indeed death, when sin happens the sinner must die. However God provided a means by which a substitute may die instead of the sinner. In the Old Testament, lambs, bulls, and goats comprised the substitute, dying in the sinner's place. The blood of the sacrifice became the atonement for the sinner (Leviticus 17:11). When the substitute died, divine justice was accomplished and God's wrath was satisfied.

What should be our response to this threat of divine wrath and judgment? First, it would be a tragic error to minimize or deny it, as though somehow God in His righteous character has changed between the day of Moses and our time. God Himself puts the lie to that in Malachi 3:6, "For I, the LORD, do not change," a point James 1:17 makes as well. The New Testament doesn't disavow God's wrath at sin or the need to satisfy it, but instead reveals that those ancient sacrifices were temporary types of the final, perfect sacrifice that was to be made by Christ, offering Himself as "the lamb of God who takes away the sins of the world" (John 1:29).

Second, it would be equally tragic to assume that the sacrifice of Christ *automatically* delivers *everyone* from judgment. This is a commonly held (but wholly mistaken) opinion in our day referred to as Universalism. The idea is that *all* men have been saved by the work of Christ, and the task of evangelism is to simply *announce* that great salvation. This is a grave error. One needs not but to read the book of Acts to see the apostles calling people to specific, intentional, individual repentance (see, for instance, Acts 16:31). Paul himself literally begs people to be reconciled to God (2 Corinthians 5:20).[9] The universalist's typical response to verses such as these runs something along the lines that *the salvation being spoken of is from a life of unhappiness, uselessness, or purposelessness*. They would say that *everyone is on the ship of salvation, we're all traveling together, but those of us who realize and live out our salvation in Christ will enjoy the trip more than those who don't.*

There are many, many places in Scripture that refute this mistaken notion, but let's glance at just one. Paul says in 2 Thessalonians 1:8-9 that the recompense to those who "do not know God and to those who do not obey the gospel of our Lord Jesus" is not that they will go through life frustrated, missing out on the joy that could be theirs, but that they "will pay the penalty of eternal destruction, away from the presence of the Lord."

---
9   Logically, Paul's statement assumes that men are *not* automatically reconciled.

Let me beg *you*, dear reader, to be reconciled to God. As the Scripture has said, you, along with the rest of us, have sinned (Romans 3:23). The deeds of your life will *not* be compared with those of other people but with what God requires, which is _perfect holiness_:

- "Speak to all the congregation of the sons of Israel and say to them, 'You shall be holy, for I the LORD your God am holy'" (Leviticus 19:2).

- "For I say to you, that unless your righteousness surpasses that of the scribes and Pharisees, you shall not enter the kingdom of heaven" (Matthew 5:20).

- "Therefore you are to be _perfect_, as your heavenly Father is perfect" (Matthew 5:48, emphasis mine).

That same wrath of which Moses writes *you* will experience if you meet God on the basis of your own deeds. Isaiah tells us that even our _righteous deeds_ are in His sight nothing more than filthy rags (Isaiah 64:6). Obviously, we can not stand in the burning presence of the holy God of the universe clothed in the filthy rags of our own self-righteousness. So what hope have we?

The hope is this: what we could neither do nor be, God sent His Son as a perfect sacrifice to do and be for us, in our place, on our behalf.[10] The perfection that God re-

---

10 And this is our only hope according to the Bible (for example, Acts 4:12). There is no hope of forgiveness other than through Christ. This is the decisive

Chapter 5: The Wrathful Judge: Condemnation (Part 2), v 7

quires Jesus attained, so much so that Paul teaches that Jesus is the "*end* of the Law to all who believe" (Romans 10:4). Not only that, but the death of Christ on the cross pays for all our sins, both those sins we have already committed as well as those we have yet to commit (Hebrews 10:11-14). His resurrection from the dead demonstrates that God has fully accepted His payment for our sin (this is what is meant by the term *propitiation* used in 1 John 2:2).

Those who place their faith in Christ and His death and resurrection for their sins are granted these twin blessings: their sins are considered as fully paid by the death of Christ, and they are credited with the perfect righteousness of Christ established by His sinless life. Those who possess these blessings are reconciled forever with God. Paul gives us a concise synopsis of this great blessing in Romans 4:5, "But to the one who does not work,[11] but believes in Him who justifies the ungodly,[12] his faith is reckoned as righteousness."[13]

Sadly, the universalists are wrong and tragically so. From the very beginning God has required a specific response of faith to what He has said. The universalists

---

testimony of Scripture.

11 In other words, makes no effort to establish personal righteousness by his own "good deeds."

12 To be justified means one has been declared righteous. In Scripture, one who is *justified* by God is *saved*, or *reconciled* to God. Against a justified one God brings no charge of sin.

13 The faith that lays hold of Christ's righteousness, rather than one's own [self-]righteousness, is *imputed* or credited as righteousness. See an explicit statement of this crediting in Romans 4:3.

are guilty not only of their sins, but worse, they are guilty for refusing to believe what God has proclaimed in His Word. They are repeating the sin of Eve, as she chose to believe the serpent over what God had unambiguously said (compare Genesis 2:17 with 3:4-6). On the final day they will awaken to the fact that, like the vast mass of unbelieving humanity, they have been traveling on that broad road leading to destruction; they have built their houses on the sand of human opinions rather than the rock of the Word of God. And on that day they will be unable to charge God with injustice; their mouths will be stopped and they will acknowledge the righteousness of God in His fiery judgment of their sins.

Let that not happen to you: *listen* to the voice of Moses in Psalm 90 and *fear* the wrath of God! Let that wise fear drive you to *accept* and *trust* God's gracious, complete, and loving provision for you: Jesus Christ and His death and resurrection, which fully satisfies the wrath of God on behalf of all those who trust in Him. Apart from responding to God by faith as He requires—no matter what you may think or might have been taught—you have no hope (Ephesians 2:12).

Chapter 5: The Wrathful Judge: Condemnation (Part 2), v 7

Food for Thought

Read Psalm 90, then focus on verse 7.

1. Other than God's condemnation of sin (v 3), what accounts for our short lives?

2. The claim was made in this chapter that the wrath of God is a significant theme of Psalm 90. Read the entire psalm and list all the points at which you see God's wrath in operation, either through direct statement or consequence.

3. How was God's wrath against sin temporarily satisfied in the Old Testament? How is it permanently satisfied in the New Testament?

4. How do you plan on satisfying God's burning anger against your sins? What confidence do you have that God will find your plan acceptable?

5. Are you afraid of God's wrath? Should you be? Why or why not?

Chapter 6: The Wrathful Judge: Sin (Part 1), vs 8-10

8 You have set our iniquities before you, our secret sins in the light of your presence.

Moses attributes God's wrath to our sin. "**Our iniquities**" and our "**secret sins**" turn out to be not-so-secret, as they are exposed "**in the light of your presence**."

The first portion of the verse speaks of God placing our sins before Him ("**set . . . before you**") such that they become the basis of His conduct toward us. "God sets transgressions before Him, when . . . He makes them an object of punishment."[1] This accounts for His burning anger (v 7).

The second portion advances the same thought by telling us that even those transgressions we thought secret serve as evidence against us, being clearly known to God. Our foolish efforts to conceal our conduct is set against the omniscient ease with which God sees through our vain attempts to hide our wickedness. Hebrews 4:13 tells us, "And there is no creature hidden from His sight, but all things are open and laid bare to the eyes of Him with whom we have to do."

This also makes obvious that God's wrath is a righteous wrath: He is judging man according to clearly manifested transgressions. He is judging us as our sins deserve! Paul says in Romans 2:5-6 , "But because of your stubbornness and unrepentant heart you are storing up

---
1   Delitzsch, 3:55.

wrath for yourself in the day of wrath and revelation of the righteous judgment of God, who will render to every man according to his deeds: . . ."

Martin Luther, in applying Psalm 90 to his own life, views "**our secret sins**" as sins that *we ourselves don't even recognize*. Like a rotten plank in the deck of a swinging bridge spanning a deep chasm, those sins we have committed and of which we are unaware are as deadly to our eternal destiny as our high-handed ones. Kidner echoes Luther when he says, "As for *our secret sins*, they must include those that we would disguise even from ourselves."[2]

According to Luther biographer Roland Bainton, Luther "was thinking of his fruitless efforts in the cloister to recall every wrongdoing, that it might be confessed and pardoned."[3] Luther was driven to near madness by the heavy conviction of sin during his days as a Roman Catholic monk. The poor monk was making the mistake of thinking it was the completeness and fervancy of his own penance that bought forgiveness. It was not until Luther understood justification by faith alone in Christ alone through God's grace alone that he was delivered from his terrified bondage.[4]

God is the Divine Searcher, who knows every secret of

---

2 Kidner, 361.
3 Roland Bainton, *Here I Stand: A Life of Martin Luther* (New York and Nashville: Abingdon, 1950): 335, quoted in C. Hassell Bullock, *Encountering the Book of Psalms* (Grand Rapids: Baker Academic, 2001), 94.
4 These were three of the Reformation *solas* that grew out of the recovery of the true gospel of Christ.

Chapter 6: The Wrathful Judge: Sin (Part 1), vs 8-10

men's hearts. Psalm 33:13-15 says, "The LORD looks from heaven; He sees all the sons of men; from His dwelling place He looks out on all the inhabitants of the earth, He who fashions the hearts of them all, He who understands all their works." Paul tells us that "God will judge the secrets of men through Christ Jesus" (Romans 2:16). Jesus said in Luke 12:2 , "But there is nothing covered up that will not be revealed, and hidden that will not be known." God is able to keep His secrets from us (Deut 29:29) but we are not able to keep ours from Him. Lewis captures something of the exposure by "**the light of [His] presence**" on the day of judgment: "In the end that Face which is the delight or terror of the universe must be turned upon each of us . . . , either conferring glory inexpressible or inflicting shame that can never be cured or disguised."[5]

We must heed the counsel of Proverbs 28:13 : "He who conceals his transgressions will not prosper, But he who confesses and forsakes them will find compassion." In view of the corruption of our own hearts (Jeremiah 17:9), we need the candle of the Holy Spirit to "search me, O God, and know my heart; Try me and know my anxious thoughts; And see if there be any hurtful way in me, And lead me in the everlasting way" (Psalm 139:23-24). Far better is it for *us* to name our sins and seek mercy in Christ, before *He* names them in

---

[5] C. S. Lewis, "The Weight of Glory", in *Transposition* (Bles, 1949): 28, quoted in Derek Kidner, *Psalms 1-72*, vol. 15 of *Tyndale Old Testament Commentaries*, ed. Donald J. Wiseman (1973; repr., Downers Grove, IL: Inter-Varsity Press, 2008), 96.

judgment on that great and terrible day. The terrifying expectation of our secret sins spread openly before the blazing holiness of God should cause us to flee to the cross and find safety in Christ.

For those who are trusting in the blood of Christ as their complete sacrifice for sin, all of their sins—known and unknown—have been fully paid by Christ and the Heavenly Father is fully satisfied with the transaction.[6] What a joy it is to know we will never face judgment, because our Savior has already been fully judged in our place! What a release from guilt and fear! This faith alone is what turned Luther from a terrified monk into the lion of the Reformation.

9 For all our days decline through your overflowing fury; we complete our years like a sigh.

Though the psalm is nothing like a formal proof, yet the psalmist does summon evidence for his assertion that our sins have been placed before God for judgment: **"For all our days decline . . . ."** God's **overflowing fury** (*'ebrah*) is the ultimate cause of our shortened life, although a variety of events may be the immediate cause (illness, car accident, etc.). Moses has an unfortunate vantage point from which he may watch the declining days of an unbelieving generation. Jeremiah had a similar position as he watched unfaithful Judah being decimated by the Babylonians. Using the same word

---

[6] The Father's satisfaction with the provision of Christ's atonement for sinners is evidenced by the resurrection of Christ. When the sin debt was completely paid, there was no longer any need to hold Him in death.

CHAPTER 6: THE WRATHFUL JUDGE: SIN (PART 1), VS 8-10

translated above as "overwhelming fury," the weeping prophet cries, "Cut off your hair and cast it away, And take up a lamentation on the bare heights; For the LORD has rejected and forsaken the generation of His wrath [*'ebrah*]"(Jeremiah 7:29).

The verb translated "**complete**" in the second portion of verse 9 is rendered "come to an end" in verse 7. The idea is that we "go out with a whimper," our "**years**" ending in unimpressive weakness or unfulfilled potential. The word translated **sigh** may be onomatopoetic: it sounds like an expired breath: *hegeh*.[7]

What a sad end for the covenant people of God, especially when considering what initial promise they had with God as their leader, guide, protector, and provider! How different might history have been, had the rebellious generation chosen a path of humble obedience?

On one hand, it seems to be a fruitless question because under God's sovereign management of the cosmos He ordains *all* that comes to pass and He obviously permitted the unbelief and wickedness of Israel to bring their great potential to nothing. On the other hand, our choices are real and consequential, and we are held accountable for them: Jesus laments over the holy city, crying out: "O Jerusalem, Jerusalem, who kills the prophets and stones those who are sent to her! *How often I wanted to gather your children together, the way*

---

[7] An onomatopoetic word is one whose pronunciation suggests its meaning. For instance, the word "*bang*!" is onomatopoetic.

a hen gathers her chicks under her wings, and you were unwilling" (Matthew 23:37, emphasis mine). This text from Matthew (and others like it) eliminates the notion that the cosmos is but a machine, grinding out the cold and inexorable fate planned for her. Is God sovereign? Certainly, and none can thwart His will! Are our choices real? Yes, and they have consequences and we will be held fully responsible! This is an antinomy: an insoluble conundrum. Though we are incapable in our creaturely logic to resolve the knot, we cannot deny the reality of either: the Bible plainly teaches *both*. The Creator/creature distinction is demonstrated in part by our inability (and *inability* it truly is) to comprehend His work in creating, ordering, and maintaining this world.

This much is clear: having redeemed His chosen people from Egypt, and having given them His Law, God *set before them* the Promised Land. They refused to go in, they disobeyed by their own choice. So God *set before Himself* their sins, and pronounced judgment: they will wander in the wilderness for forty years; not one man of that generation will enter into the Promised Land, save Joshua and Caleb (Numbers 14:30). Now, as they wander and watch friends, neighbors, and family members succumb to the judgment of death, Moses writes that they have "come to an end by your anger" and "our days decline through your overflowing fury" and "we complete our years like a sigh."

There are many causes behind suffering in this fallen

CHAPTER 6: THE WRATHFUL JUDGE: SIN (PART 1), VS 8-10

world. For the covenant child of God our suffering sometimes is not due to sin but to righteousness, as was the case with Job.[8] Peter tells us that godly suffering will result in opportunities to spread the Gospel (1 Peter 3:15). Jesus speaks of a case of suffering that was explicitly designed to reveal the glory of God (John 9:3). But it is also true that suffering can come as a result of our own sinful choices that are counter to God's will and holiness as revealed in the Bible.

The specific reference to which Psalm 90:9 points is the consequence suffered by the children of Israel due to their rebellion against God. But more widely, the verse refers to the general condition of life in a fallen world.

10 The days of our life are seventy years, or if due to strength, eighty years, though their best is but trouble and sorrow, for it passes quickly and we fly away.

> *Time, like an ever rolling stream,*
> *Bears all its sons away;*
> *They fly, forgotten, as a dream*
> *Dies at the opening day.*[9]

Remember: this is poetry. Moses is not intending to give a precise life-span; he is positing an unremarkable

---
[8] The trials Job experienced were explicitly due to his faithfulness in serving God. See Job 1—Satan's challenges were provoked through God's testimony of Job's *righteousness*.
[9] Watts, v. 7.

average, and then extending it by ten years in the case of those who possess unusual vigor. How man's weakness is underscored by this verse! The *mighty God* (*'el*, v 2) is from everlasting to everlasting; the *mighty man* may add a piddling ten years to his lifespan, before coming to an end like a sigh. What a contrast! The point is that of brevity which, even at its best, is marked by trouble: "For affliction does not come from the dust, Neither does trouble sprout from the ground, For man is born for trouble, As sparks fly upward" (Job 5:6-7).

"**Their best**" is literally *their pride* and refers to the best years, the years of a man in his strength and prime. Yet even those good years are marked by trouble or suffering. The noun "**trouble**" (*'amal*) is often employed in its verb form to speak of drudgery and toil (as opposed to work that is rewarding). It is a word used frequently by Qoheleth[10] in Ecclesiastes to speak of laborious toil "under the sun." Here in Psalm 90:10 it is associated with "sorrow." Elsewhere it is coupled with "torment" or "sorrow" (Je 20:18), "vexation" (Psalm 10:14), "affliction" and "oppression" (Deut 26:7), "vanity" (Job 7:3), "violence" or "destruction" (Proverbs 24:2), etc.[11] BDB indicates that it often refers to personal suffering.[12]

---

10 The jury is still out on the authorship of Ecclesiastes. Many now consider the book to be somewhat of an envelope structure, with the opening and closing words by Solomon, sandwiching the words of Qoheleth (an unnamed preacher). I'm inclined to believe the whole thing is by Solomon, but I admit to the uncertainty. In any case, it is inspired Scripture.
11 Ronald B. Allen, in TWOT, 1639a.
12 The *Brown, Driver, and Briggs Hebrew Lexicon*, a standard tool for Hebrew

CHAPTER 6: THE WRATHFUL JUDGE: SIN (PART 1), VS 8-10

The noun "**sorrow**" (*'aven*) is virtually synonymous in meaning to "trouble" (*'amal*), and has reference here to the sorrow that results from the trouble of living in a fallen world. Moses, therefore, confesses in his prayer that man's pride, even his very best, is unalterably associated with **trouble** and stained by **sorrow**.

"**For it passes quickly**," referring to the span of our life, "**and we fly away**," seems to point to an image of the soul departing the body, much as Rachel's soul departed as she gave birth to Benjamin in Genesis 35:18. Coincidentally, she named him Ben-oni, "son of my sorrow" (*'aven*).[13]

Verse 10 reinforces the temporary, transitory quality of our lives which at their best remain sullied with trouble, sorrow, and sin. Jacob's testimony to Pharaoh is telling: "And Jacob said unto Pharaoh, 'The days of the years of my pilgrimage are an hundred and thirty years: few and evil have the days of the years of my life been . . .'" (Genesis 47:9, KJV). While on the one hand we might be tempted to label such a glum testimony as a "glass half-empty" sort of perspective, on the other hand it highlights the truth of the difficulty of living in a fallen world. Better off is the man who is in touch with his own sinfulness, and the fallenness of the world around him, than the man who is glibly able to overlook both. Since it is the sick who seek the services of the physician, not the well, it is best we know the reality of our

---
studies.
13 Jacob renamed him "Benjamin," meaning "son of the right hand."

condition while there is yet time to seek Christ. Perhaps this is what Qoheleth had in mind when he wrote:

> "It is better to go to a house of mourning than to go to a house of feasting, because that is the end of every man, and the living takes it to heart. . . . The mind of the wise is in the house of mourning, while the mind of fools is in the house of pleasure" (Ecclesiastes 7:2-4).

Food for Thought

Read Psalm 90, then focus on verses 8-10.

1. Have you ever done something and learned only much later that God considered it a sin? What can you do about "secret sins" of which you are unaware?

2. Is ignorance an acceptable excuse in the court of God? Does it absolve the ignorant one of responsibility? Before you answer, contrast Ephesians 4:17-18 with Luke 12:47-48.

3. Can you identify with the sense of gloom that pervades verses 8-10? What have you seen in your own life that reinforces the reality of your own fallenness and the fallenness of the world in which you live?

4. If you are at all familiar with the Bible, you know that hope is offered through Christ. Why do you think the Spirit of God is focusing so relentlessly on our failures in this Psalm? Why not skip all this and go directly to, say, verse 14? Is it because Psalm 90 is an Old Testament text and Christ has not yet appeared, or is there something else at work?

Chapter 7: The Wrathful Judge: Sin (Part 2), v 11

11 Who knows the strength of your anger, or your overflowing fury according to the fear due you?

Like a symphony which reaches its climax in the final movement, Psalm 90's theme of God's wrath reaches its terrifying height in verse 11. The remainder of the psalm moves into a hope-filled resolution of the thematic tension of God's righteous anger. We must, however, pass through the crescendo of Moses' exploration of God's wrath before we can adequately appreciate the hope that is offered.

Verse 11 contains powerful irony when set against Moses' own personal experience. Moses asks, rhetorically, "**who knows the strength of your anger** [*'aph*]?" The implication is that *no one* knows the strength of God's anger. And yet Moses has been a first-hand witness of some of the most frightening examples of God's anger and overflowing fury contained in the Bible. For the reader, the question could be rephrased, "If not even *Moses* knows the strength of God's anger, who does?"

Moses had seen God's anger exercised against Pharaoh and Egypt. The plague on the night of the Passover (the death of the first-born son) was a severe judgment, worse than all the other plagues. The annihilation of the Egyptian army in the swirling waters of the Red Sea was a regional catastrophe; coming on the heels of the deaths of the first-born, the deaths of so many more fathers and sons must have been horrific. Yet even those events don't plumb the depths of God's righteous wrath!

Moses had witnessed God's wrath break out among God's own people in their many instances of grumbling and complaining. The slaughter of three thousand idolaters at the foot of Mount Sinai (Exodus 32:28) was but a harbinger of both the Israelites' proclivity to sin and God's fierce anger as a consequence. The warning of Exodus 33:3, 5 was explicit: " . . . I will not go up in your midst, because you are an obstinate people, and *I might destroy you on the way*. . . . should I go up in your midst for one moment, *I would destroy you*."

When Nadab and Abihu, God's chosen priests, offered incense in a self-willed, self-styled manner of worship fire came out from the presence of the Lord and *destroyed them* in an instant (Leviticus 10:1-3). Apparently God does not do nepotism, because these were Aaron's sons, Moses' nephews, and yet they suffered His judgment!

In the careful instructions Moses was given for the Day of Atonement, even the High Priest must follow to the letter the procedure prescribed, "*or he will die*" (Leviticus 16:2, 13). When Aaron and Miriam murmured against Moses, effectively questioning God's choice of a leader and His administration through Moses, Miriam was judged with leprosy (Numbers 12); only Moses' intervention saved her. When the spies delivered a frightening report of the Promised Land and a rebellion

CHAPTER 7: THE WRATHFUL JUDGE: SIN (PART 2), V 11

against God and against Moses resulted, God condemned an *entire generation* to death in the wilderness (Numbers 14:28-35). When Korah, Dathan, Abiram, and On led a rebellion against Moses' leadership, accusing him of exalting himself above the assembly of the Lord (Numbers 16), Moses witnessed the earth "open its mouth" and swallow them up. The following day Israel grumbled against Moses as though he, and not the Lord, had effected the judgment. In response to their grumbling God sent a plague that destroyed another 14,700 people. And as our final example (there could be many more) Moses himself committed a sin of disobedience, and was judged: he would not be allowed to enter the Promised Land (Numbers 20:12).

The irony is that Moses had witnessed God's fierce, burning anger many times and yet he still does not know **the strength of** [His] **anger**. If Moses doesn't, no one does! None can stand before God's wrath; His judgments against sin and rebellion are wholly righteous *and* completely devastating. Here in Psalm 90:11, Moses confesses the *overwhelming power* of God's fury unleashed.

"Who knows . . . **your overflowing fury according to the fear due you**?" This is a difficult sentence to translate. Some of the more common translations have rendered it as follows:

- Psalm 90:11 (NASB): Who understands the power of Thine anger, **And Thy fury,**

according to the fear that is due Thee?

- Psalm 90:11 (ASV): Who knoweth the power of thine anger, **And thy wrath according to the fear that is due unto thee?**

- Psalm 90:11 (NIV): Who knows the power of your anger? **For your wrath is as great as the fear that is due you.**

- Psalm 90:11 (NLT): Who can comprehend the power of your anger? **Your wrath is as awesome as the fear you deserve.**

- Psalm 90:11 (KJV): Who knoweth the power of thine anger? **even according to thy fear, so is thy wrath.**

- Psalm 90:11 (RSV): Who considers the power of thy anger, **and thy wrath according to the fear of thee?**

- Psalm 90:11 (ESV): Who considers the power of your anger, **and your wrath according to the fear of you?**

- Psalm 90:11 (NET): Who can really fathom the intensity of your anger? **Your raging fury causes people to fear you.**

A wooden translation yields: "Who knows strength anger of you, or according to your fear your

CHAPTER 7: THE WRATHFUL JUDGE: SIN (PART 2), V 11

overflowing fury."[1] The emphasis is on the fear that *we should have* of God's overflowing fury. The second portion borrows its main verb from the first, resulting in: "*Who knows your overflowing fury according to the fear due you?*" The implication is astounding: as much as we fear God and His overflowing fury, *we don't fear Him as we ought!* We don't fear Him with the fear *due* Him. The fear due Him is not simply a reflection of His great majesty and divine sovereignty, though that is surely the case. Rather, the fear due Him is to be commensurate with His overflowing fury at sin, a wrath of which we cannot plumb the depths.

And to turn the argument somewhat on its head, we should remember that God's wrath arises from His offended holiness. If we don't know the depth of His wrath, it follows that neither do we know the heights of His holiness!

Properly understanding Psalm 90 and its focus on the wrath of God is crucial for combating one of the greatest challenges that Christianity in America faces at the present time. There is a danger growing inside evangelical churches: attenders for whom God's wrath and God's holiness are no longer truths worthy of serious

---

[1] A "wooden" translation maintains, as much as possible, word order and basic word meaning as presented in the original. However, that does not mean that a wooden translation accurately conveys the meaning. Re-arrangement must take place to compensate for the difference in word order, idiom, etc. between the source language (Hebrew) and the target language (in our case, English). Remember, a Hebrew reader of Psalm 90 does not read it as a wooden statement, but as an artfully-constructed poetic assertion.

contemplation. These people have confessed a Christ but it is a truncated Christ who bears little resemblance to the Redeemer of Scripture. Their god is a god who affirms their basic goodness, who desires that they be "nice" (rather than holy), who helps them with self-improvement and self-actualization, and yet remains comfortably distant and uninvolved in matters such as genuine social justice, sexual morality, honesty in tax-reporting, purity in communications, etc. This god makes very few demands and whenever he rebukes them for being "not nice" he does it with a wink and a nod and a twinkle in his grandfatherly eye.

A term has been coined for this distinctly American version of Christianity: Moralistic Therapeutic Deism, or MTD.[2] Al Mohler, commenting on the god of MTD, says, "this deity does not challenge the most basic self-centered assumptions of our postmodern age. Particularly when it comes to so-called 'lifestyle' issues, this God is exceedingly tolerant and this religion is radically undemanding."[3] Mohler's assessment of the impact of MTD on biblical Christianity is striking:

> "This radical transformation of Christian theology and Christian belief replaces the sovereignty of God with the sovereignty of the self. In this therapeutic age, human problems are

---

[2] Coined by researchers Christian Smith and Melinda Lundquist Denton in their ground-breaking book, *Soul Searching: The Religious and Spiritual Lives of American Teenagers*, Oxford University Press, 2005.

[3] Al Mohler, http://www.christianpost.com/news/moralistic-therapeutic-deism-the-new-american-religion-6266/, accessed 2/8/2012.

reduced to pathologies in need of a treatment plan. Sin is simply excluded from the picture, and doctrines as central as the wrath and justice of God are discarded as out of step with the times and unhelpful to the project of self-actualization."[4]

Grasping the depth of the wrath of God, presented by Moses in Psalm 90 as something far greater than mankind is able to comprehend, is the antidote to a corrupted Christianity that no longer requires the cross because the people it redeems are no longer helplessly evil but merely in need of improvement. Psalm 111:9-10 (emphasis mine) conjoins the holiness of God with the fear of God:

> He has sent redemption to His people; He has ordained His covenant forever; *Holy and awesome is His name. The fear of the* LORD *is the beginning of wisdom*; A good understanding have all those who do His commandments; His praise endures forever.

There are, then, two points we as readers must consider: first, we *ought* to fear God and His almighty wrath. It is the starting point of wisdom. There is a fear *due* Him, and it's not *pro forma*, but a genuine terror of God's wrath should it be unleashed. Second, we cannot fathom the magnitude of God's anger against the sin that daily offends His holiness. The power of God's an-

---

[4] *Ibid.*

ger:

> [J]ust happens to be the one truth that men do not regard. Life could not be the futile thing that it is if God were not thoroughly displeased with men. No other force could reduce life to the level on which it is lived.[5]

The Book of Revelation displays the cup of God's wrath being poured out upon a Christ-rejecting world:

> And the sky was split apart like a scroll when it is rolled up; and every mountain and island were moved out of their places. And the kings of the earth and the great men and the commanders and the rich and the strong and every slave and free man, hid themselves in the caves and among the rocks of the mountains; and they said to the mountains and to the rocks, "Fall on us and hide us from the presence of Him who sits on the throne, *and from the wrath of the Lamb; for the great day of their wrath has come; and who is able to stand?*" (Revelation 6:14-17, emphasis mine).

An even clearer picture is displayed for us on the cross, where God poured out His wrath on His own Son, the sin-bearer (Isaiah 53:6) for all who will call upon Him. Jesus' cry of dereliction reveals the Father's surging anger against the sins of mankind: "My God! My God!

---
5   Leupold, 646-7.

Why have you forsaken me?" (Matthew 27:46). God's righteous wrath against sin is so consuming that no propitiation short of the blood of His own divine Son is able to satisfy it.

Food for Thought

Read Psalm 90, then focus on verse 11.

1. Why is verse 11 all the more shocking when you consider who wrote it?

2. What were some of the ways that Moses was acquainted with the strength of God's anger?

3. Does anyone truly know the depth of God's anger at sin? Support your answer from Psalm 90.

4. What is the connection between God's holiness and His wrath at sin? If we downplay His wrath, how might that affect our apprehension of His holiness?

5. The frightening news of God's wrath has often been lost in the proclamation of His mercy. What impact does that have on the message of the gospel and the holiness of the church?

Chapter 8: Our Response to God's Wrath, v 12

12 So teach us to number our days that we may gain a heart of wisdom.

Because of God's righteous wrath against sin Moses prays that God might give His people hearts trained to consider their own mortality, so that they may learn wisdom. The form of the request is eloquent: "**teach us to number our days**". Luther translates this in a characteristically blunt fashion: "Teach us to reflect on death that we may be wise."[1]

"Teach us" is literally, "cause us to know," or "make known to us." The problem—sin—is ours. The solution, however, is not something within ourselves; the solution is God's. We have placed ourselves into a dilemma we cannot fix; it must be fixed for us. Moses, the great intercessor, asks *God* to be the solution ("*cause* us to know"), to be the Divine Teacher who will impart the truth that sets us free. Moses is praying for divine intervention that impacts us at all points of our corruption: our will, intellect, and emotions.

The Bible unfolds in precise terms the spiritual impact of sin, but it is a diagnosis with which many moderns are uncomfortable and most frankly reject. If given the opportunity to choose the metaphor best portraying the human spiritual condition, most would pick the image

---
1 Roland Bainton, *Here I Stand: A Life of Martin Luther* (New York and Nashville: Abingdon, 1950): 335, quoted in C. Hassell Bullock, *Encountering the Book of Psalms* (Grand Rapids: Baker Academic, 2001), 94.

of an injured person in a wheelchair rather than a corpse in a casket. The need, modern man would say, is for strengthening and improvement, not total re-creation. Put another way, our culture believes that man's need can be answered through therapy; wholesale regeneration is not required.

However, the Bible reveals the sinner not as weak but as truly dead in trespasses and sins (Ephesians 2:1) and in need of an entirely new life (2 Corinthians 5:17). As a dead man, the sinner is incapable of the sort of moral improvement favored by religion. Consider the following assertions about the natural state of man.

- His heart is corrupted beyond his capacity to understand, Jeremiah 17:9.

- Even his best deeds are considered sinful by God, Isaiah 64:6.

- He consciously suppresses the truth about God, Romans 1:18.

- He has traded truth about God for a lie, Romans 1:25a.

- Rejecting the Creator, he has chosen instead to worship the creation, Romans 1:25b.

- He does not seek after the true God, Romans 3:11.

- By virtue of his rebellion he has become worthless, Romans 3:12.

- He is in bondage to sin, Romans 6:20; 7:14.
- Nothing good dwells within him, Romans 7:18.
- He is implacably hostile against the true God, Romans 8:7; Colossians 1:21.
- He is incapable of pleasing the true God, Romans 8:8.
- He is unable to understand spiritual truth, 1 Corinthians 2:14.
- He is dead in trespasses and sins, Ephesians 2:1.
- His heart is filled with corrupting wickedness, Mark 7:21-23.
- He can not come to Christ unless drawn by the Father, John 6:44.

These are not rhetorical or hyperbolic statements, but are clear-eyed assessments by the Spirit of God revealing the human condition as it actually is. In such a state of affairs if anyone at all is to be redeemed God must make it happen. He must provide a means of atonement for sin, and then must work sovereignly in the will of the sinner to cause him or her to seek redemption. This necessarily means that God overrides man's hostility, overrides his sinful inclination to reject truth, and grants to that sinner genuine repentance and saving faith. The gospel, which has been held by the sinner to be utter foolishness, must be revealed to sin-blinded eyes as a message of surpassing value. Whereas the sinner formerly viewed Jesus as a religious figure and perhaps even a religious personage of note, God must enlighten the eyes such that "the light of the knowledge of the glory of God *in the face of Christ*" can be clearly seen (2 Corinthians 4:6, emphasis mine). Jonah's statement in the belly of the great fish sums up the divine role: "Salvation is from the LORD" (Jonah 2:8).

These are things God and God alone can accomplish, and apart from His sovereign doing of them the sinner will be separated from God for eternity with no hope of reconciliation. *Never* will a sin-blinded, spiritually dead, hostile sinner seek the Lord on his own. This is why Moses prays "teach us" or "cause us to know." He seeks the divine intervention of Yahweh, who has already acted sovereignly on behalf of His covenant people with respect to their deliverance from Egypt. Now Moses prays that they would be delivered from themselves.

Rather than being uncomfortable with God's sovereignty in salvation we should be thankful for it. Repentance is a gift from God according to Acts 11:18. Because repentance and faith are two sides to the same coin, faith must also be a gift from God. Paul verifies this in Philippians 1:29 when he mentions in an aside (as he pursues a different argument) that belief in Christ has been "granted" to the Philippians.

Sin is so corrupting that we will never—can never—come to God on our own. Moses says, *cause* us to know. Moses pleads for God's sovereign intervention in the hearts of His hopelessly rebellious people. We see this prayer answered in God the Father's unilateral act of drawing sinners to His Son (John 6:44).

If we **number our days**, reflecting on the fact that death and judgment approach, we will learn the fear of God. Proverbs 9:10 asserts that the proper fear of the Lord (of which Moses speaks in Psalm 90:11) is *the beginning of wisdom*. Knowing the fear that is due God by virtue of the power of His disapproval is the first step of **gaining a heart of wisdom**.

Wisdom in the Old Testament could be characterized as the *daily outworking of the reflection of God's own holiness in the lives of His covenant people*. God demands that His people model holiness in all aspects of life. In the book of Job wisdom is presented as a divine attribute: "With Him are wisdom and might; To Him belong counsel and understanding" (Job 12:13). Job tells his friends that God alone knows wisdom: "Where then does wisdom come from? And where is the place of understanding? . . . . God understands its way; And He knows its place" (Job 28:20, 23).

Uniquely vivid among the portrayals of wisdom in the ancient Near East, Proverbs personifies wisdom as a woman (Proverbs 8, 9:1-6), stopping just short of claiming actual personhood for it. Wisdom was brought forth before Creation (Proverbs 8:22-31) and teaches in public places (Proverbs 8:1-6). She is contrasted with Dame Folly (Proverbs 9:13-18).

Knowing that the days which we are given to "gain a heart of wisdom" are not limitless, but are numbered, should provide us with the proper perspective for the pursuit of wisdom. As Jesus said,

> "Take heed, keep on the alert; for you do not know when the appointed time is. It is like a man, away on a journey, who upon leaving his house and putting his slaves in charge, assigning to each one his task, also commanded the doorkeeper to stay on the alert. Therefore, be on the alert—for you do not know when the master of the house is coming, whether in the evening, at midnight, at cockcrowing, or in the morning — lest he come suddenly and find you asleep. And what I say to you I say to all, 'Be on the alert!'" (Mark 13:33-37)

What Moses is asking for, then, is a sovereignly provided, clear-headed perspective on our mortality that will impact the way we think about life and the way we live it. Our accountability to our Creator needs to become the lens through which we view everything else. Bullock's general comment on Psalm 90 is helpful: "This psalm has a way of calming the soul. When human beings have a sense of their tenuous place in the universe and their transitory existence, they need to see themselves in view of the God of time and eternity."[2]

Consequently, we must consider our time and the use of it with eternity in view. We must invest it wisely, making Christ-honoring decisions so that we bring not only broken and contrite hearts before Him, but hearts made wise as well. "A wise heart is the fruit which one reaps or garners in from such numbering of the days, the gain which one carries off from so constantly reminding one's self of the end."[3]

This is the thrust of Qoheleth in the conclusion of Ecclesiastes:

> "The conclusion, when all has been heard, is: fear God and keep His commandments, because this applies to every person. For God will bring every act to judgment, everything which is hidden, whether it is good or evil" (Ecclesiastes 12:13-14).

Jesus Christ is revealed in the New Testament as the One to which all the Old Testament wisdom types point. Paul says that Christ *is* the wisdom of God (1 Corinthians 1:24, 30). In the end, to gain a heart of wisdom we must gain Christ.

---

[2] Bullock, 174.
[3] Delitzsch, 3:58.

Food for Thought

Read Psalm 90, then focus on verse 12.

1. Write down what you have learned so far from Psalm 90.

2. How has your knowledge of God been refined, or perhaps even changed?

3. How has your evaluation of yourself changed?

4. What does Moses ask for in verse 12, and what is his reason?

5. What do you think Paul means in his statements in 1 Corinthians 1:24, 30, to the effect that *Christ is the wisdom of God*?

6. What do you need to do now, in view of God's wrath, your sin, and the shortness of your life?

Chapter 9: A Plea for Covenant Compassion, v 13

13 Return, O Lord; how long? Have compassion on your servants!

Imagine a courtroom scene in which the defendant stands charged with multiple counts of the most serious crimes against the state. The indictment is read, the charges enumerated, the list of offenses seems to go on forever. In the face of overwhelming evidence against him the accused pleads guilty to each charge. You are watching, expecting that the defendant will get the book thrown at him, for he surely deserves it.

The judge asks him if he has anything to say. He stands and says, "Your Honor, you've seen my crimes, my insurrections, my seditions against the government. In spite of all that I beg for the compassion of this court. I ask that the court would grant to me the greatest blessings the state can provide. I would like to be joyful and wake up singing every morning. Moreover, I am asking the court that my life go on record as having counted for something good that will endure forever."

You would be shocked! How can this guilty criminal ask for such things? And yet this is what Moses does, beginning in verse 13. Using a string of imperatives Moses lays his petition before the Lord, the backdrop of acknowledged human guilt notwithstanding. Moses has no *right* to ask for these blessings, but he does have something much more compelling than a right. The prophet is calling on the *covenant faithfulness* of God.

A PRAYER OF MOSES

We won't be able to understand this last portion of the psalm apart from an understanding of the covenant relationship God has with Israel, for it is to this relationship Moses appeals.

Genesis 12:1-3 is where God's special covenant relationship with the children of Israel begins to unfold. God promises Abram[1] that from his offspring He will make a great nation and will bless him, making his name great. According to the terms of the covenant all who bless Abram will themselves be blessed and those who curse him will be cursed. This promise is the *Abrahamic Covenant*. It is stated in great detail with explicit covenant terminology in Genesis 17. In Genesis 26:2-5, the covenant is passed along to Abraham's heir, Isaac, and then to his son Jacob in Genesis 28:1-4, 13-15. Jacob is renamed *Israel* in Genesis 32:28 (see also 35:9-12) and his progeny become known as the *children of Israel*, or the *sons of Israel*.

The book of Genesis closes with the sons of Israel prospering in Goshen, a territory of Egypt. God had used Joseph—a son of Jacob—to bless Egypt, averting widespread starvation by storing up food against a divinely foretold famine. The book of Exodus continues the story with these ominous words: "Now a new king arose over Egypt, who did not know Joseph" (Exodus 1:8). The king, Pharaoh, enslaved the children of Israel and treated them cruelly. This is the situation, then,

---

[1] Renamed "Abraham" in Genesis 17:5.

when we read these words:

> "Now it came about in the course of those many days that the king of Egypt died. And the sons of Israel sighed because of the bondage, and they cried out; and their cry for help because of their bondage rose up to God. So God heard their groaning; and *God remembered His covenant with Abraham, Isaac, and Jacob*" (Exodus 2:23-24, emphasis mine).

God begins to move to keep His covenant promises. What does He do? He raises up Moses to be His chosen deliverer. Moses' life and ministry is to be understood in terms of God's covenant promises. The message Moses is to bring is in the Name of the "God of Abraham, Isaac, and Jacob," an expression that alludes to the Abrahamic Covenant wherever the formula appears.[2] Through Moses God delivers an expansion on the Abrahamic Covenant in the form of the Law (which we call the *Mosaic Covenant* or the *Old Covenant*). In it God identifies Israel as His chosen people and enjoins them to keep His commandments, and they respond by promising obedience (Exodus 19:3-8; 24:3-8).

But the Law of Moses comes with its own promises, including blessings for obedience and curses for disobedience (Deuteronomy 28), and herein is the

---

[2] It appears twelve times in the Old Testament, plus three more times in the form, "the God of Abraham, the God of Isaac, and the God of Jacob." Of the total of fifteen times this formula appears, all but two are found in Exodus and Deuteronomy.

dilemma of Moses' prayer. When Israel's sin demands punishment under the terms of the covenant, how can Moses plead for blessings, especially after admitting Israel's guilt? God's own law specifies that sin shall be punished! How can God bless a sinful people without doing injury to His righteousness and justice?

The answer is found in the idea of substitutionary sacrifice. The Law makes gracious provision for the sinner to be forgiven through the atonement of a sacrifice. An innocent lamb may be slain in place of judgment falling on the sinner. The Law says, "the life of the flesh is in the blood, and I have given it to you on the altar to make atonement for your souls; for it is the blood by reason of the life that makes atonement" (Leviticus 17:11). But how can the death of an animal really cover, or atone for, the sin of a human? It can't—not in and of itself (Hebrews 10:4). God accepted it as *a divinely-appointed temporary measure that is pointing to the true sacrifice to come*, that of Jesus Christ. The efficacy is of Christ, not the lamb. This is that to which John the Baptist referred when he pointed out Jesus and said, "Behold, the Lamb of God who takes away the sin of the world" (John 1:29). Hebrews 9-10 are all about the final sacrifice, Christ, who has provided the perfect and complete atonement with His own blood. The Old Covenant sacrifices simply pointed forward in anticipation of the final, perfect, complete sacrifice of Christ Himself.

Herein is one of the most significant points of Psalm

90. In order to make the jump from declaring God's wrath to boldly seeking God's blessings, *Moses has to be anticipating a sacrifice that satisfies the terms of the covenant*. No other explanation makes sense. On one level, then, Psalm 90 contains a New Testament—or New Covenant, if you will—message: on what grounds can I, a sinner deserving divine wrath, ask for God's blessings? I can seek such only on the grounds that Christ has paid for my sins with His atoning death, fully satisfying the demands of divine justice, and has elevated me to a place of divine favor by His resurrection and ascension. Without the cross divine mercy would trivialize divine holiness and mock divine justice, but with the cross God's holiness and justice *calls for His gracious mercy toward His elect*! Why? Because the sin debt has been paid!

Using the personal name of God, **Yahweh**,[3] Moses reminds the Lord that he is asking on behalf of "**your servants**," a status God granted to Israel when He chose them as His special people and forged His covenant with them (see Exodus 19:4-6).

Moses' cry for the Lord to "**return**" echoes God's command "return" in verse 3. He is asking God to relent in his fiery judgment. In view of God's sentencing of an entire generation of Israelites to die in the desert (Num-

---

[3] Bullock makes the point that according to Jewish tradition, the name *'Elohim* denoted God's mighty sovereign transcendence, while *Yahweh* spoke of God's "compassion and personal presence," in other words, His immanence (Bullock, 126). This tradition fits well what we see in Psalm 90.

bers 14) and the announcement of judgment on Moses himself (Numbers 20:12), Moses' plea is a natural request. Exodus 32:11-14 has a similar request that God turn[4] from His anger, and significantly, it contains a covenant allusion:

> Then Moses entreated the LORD his God, and said, "O LORD, why doth Thine anger burn against Thy people whom Thou hast brought out from the land of Egypt with great power and with a mighty hand? Why should the Egyptians speak, saying, 'With evil intent He brought them out to kill them in the mountains and to destroy them from the face of the earth'? *Turn from Thy burning anger* and change Thy mind about doing harm to Thy people. *Remember Abraham, Isaac, and Israel,* Thy servants to whom Thou didst swear by Thyself, and didst say to them, '*I will multiply your descendants as the stars of the heavens, and all this land of which I have spoken I will give to your descendants, and they shall inherit it forever.*'" So the LORD changed His mind about the harm which He said He would do to His people. (Exodus 32:11-14, emphasis mine)

"**How long**" is an elliptical question: "how long will you be angry?" The ellipsis heightens the emotion, as though the questioner is so overcome he is unable to

---

[4] The Hebrew verbs "turn" in Exodus 32:12 and "return" in Psalm 90:13 are the same.

complete his query. What follows ("**Have compassion . . .**") is boldness empowered by the knowledge of God's promises. It's as though Moses had a sneak preview of Hebrews 4:16: "Let us therefore draw near with confidence to the throne of grace, that we may receive mercy and may find grace to help in time of need."

In the second portion of this verse, Moses respectfully requests, "**Have compassion on your servants.**"[5] The same verb appears in Deuteronomy 32:36, "the LORD . . . will have compassion on His servants. . . ."[6] It is also used in the Isaianic annunciation of the Messiah:

> "'Comfort, O comfort My people,' says your God. 'Speak kindly to Jerusalem; And call out to her, that her warfare has ended, that her iniquity has been removed, that she has received of the LORD's hand double for all her sins'" (Isaiah 40:1-2).[7]

When God passed before Moses in Exodus 34:6-7, compassion was the leading expression in His self-revelation:

> Then the LORD passed by in front of him and proclaimed, "The LORD, the LORD God, compassionate and gracious, slow to anger, and abounding in lovingkindness and truth; who keeps lovingkindness for thousands, who

---
5 The verb is in the imperative aspect
6 Although with a different stem, hitpael as opposed to nifal.
7 Piel stem.

forgives iniquity, transgression and sin; yet He will by no means leave the guilty unpunished, visiting the iniquity of fathers on the children and on the grandchildren to the third and fourth generations."[8]

Compassion is the tender mercy of God expressed on His elect, with particular view to our weakness as creatures. Asaph says, in Psalm 78:38-39:

"But He, being compassionate, forgave their iniquity, and did not destroy them; And often He restrained His anger, And did not arouse all His wrath. Thus He remembered that they were but flesh, a wind that passes and does not return."[9]

Moses prophesies of a future captivity and encourages God's people to seek Him, relying upon His compassion:

"But from there you will seek the LORD your God, and you will find Him if you search for Him with all your heart and all your soul. When you are in distress and all these things have come upon you, in the latter days, you will return to the LORD your God and listen to His voice. For the LORD your God is a compassionate God; He will not fail you nor

---

8   The Hebrew term translated "compassionate" is a synonym of the word "compassion" used in Psalm 90.
9   The Hebrew term translated "compassionate" is a synonym of the word "compassion" used in Psalm 90.

destroy you nor forget the covenant with your fathers which He swore to them" (Deuteronomy 4:29-31).[10]

In the parable of the prodigal son—the ultimate story of turning and returning—the compassion of the father is explicit: "And he got up and came to his father. But while he was still a long way off, his father saw him, and felt compassion for him, and ran and embraced him, and kissed him" (Luke 15:20).

And is not Moses' cry on our lips as well, as we pray for the Kingdom of Jesus Christ to come and put an end to the sin, suffering, heartache and injustice of this fallen world? Jesus is the ultimate answer to Moses' prayer that God have compassion upon His servants: "And seeing the multitudes, He felt compassion for them, because they were distressed and downcast like sheep without a shepherd" (Matthew 9:36).

---

10 The Hebrew term translated "compassionate" is a synonym of the word "compassion" used in Psalm 90.

Food for Thought

Read Psalm 90, then focus on verse 13.

1. What is compassion, as God expresses it?

2. Why is it necessary to understand Psalm 90 in terms of "covenant"?

3. Moses admits in verse 8 that God's wrath is a consequence of their sin. So on what grounds can he possibly ask for compassion? How can the demands of divine justice be served by compassion in the light of their sins?

4. List every example that comes to mind of divine compassion being expressed by Jesus Christ in the Gospels.

5. "How long?" The fact that this expression is elliptical (incomplete) gives the reader the opportunity to apply the plea to his own situation. What are some situations of difficulty in which you have wondered, "how long will this trial last?"

6. For what do you hope? What sustains you in these times of trial?

Chapter 10: A Plea for Covenant Lovingkindness (Part 1), v 14

14 Satisfy us in the morning with your lovingkindness, that we may cry out with joy and rejoice for all of our days.

> *O God, our help in ages past,*
> *Our hope for years to come,*
> *Be Thou our God while life shall last,*
> *And our eternal home.*[1]

The direction that Moses' prayer now takes hinges on what he means when he speaks of God's **lovingkindness**. The word is *ḥesed*, and while there is wide agreement as to its basic import—it speaks of God's mercy and love and is often translated *lovingkindness*—there is some disagreement about its particular object. The contention has to do with whether it refers to lovingkindness *specifically associated with a covenant between God and the recipient*, or whether it refers to lovingkindness expressed generally as part of God's goodness, without regard to one's relation to Him. The former would see God's *ḥesed* as something He showers on the elect; the latter would see it as something God grants both to the elect and to all creation.[2]

The context of Psalm 90 is overwhelmingly covenantal. While the malady of sin and the brevity of life it produces is shared by all humanity, Moses is interceding

---

1 Watts, v. 9.
2 This is effectively the distinction between "special grace" and "common grace."

for those in covenant with God. There are several lines of evidence that demand this:

- v 1: "You have been our dwelling place" - this is only true of God's elect.

- v 7: "we have come to an end" - Moses does not speak of "we" as *all humanity*; these are prayers and intercessions for the people of God whom he is leading. So with all the first-person plural references in this psalm.

- vs 13 and 16: "your servants" - Moses speaks of Israel as God's servants (see Leviticus 25:55); theologically this is not an expression that applies generally to all people.

- Psalm 90 belongs to the historical context of the deliverance God effected through Moses when He delivered His people from Egypt. This was a *covenant* deliverance: "so God heard their groaning; and *God remembered His covenant* with Abraham, Isaac, and Jacob" (Exodus 2:24, emphasis mine).

Therefore God's **lovingkindness** in Psalm 90 refers to God's special care for His chosen people, not His general care for all creation. God does love and provide for all His creatures, nonetheless He does not deliver them all from judgment.

Moses witnessed God satisfying the hunger and thirst of

CHAPTER 10: A PLEA FOR COVENANT LOVINGKINDNESS (PART 1), V 14

the children of Israel with manna, with quail, and with water from the rock. In the dry and dusty wilderness wandering God's provision preserved their lives. But they were a nation of rebels, stiff-necked in posture and rebellious in heart against all that God required.[3] Through the Law God had provided His people a means of dealing with such sinful rebellion by the sacrifice of an innocent animal: "For the life of the flesh is in the blood, and I have given it to you on the altar to make atonement for your souls; for it is the blood by reason of the life that makes atonement" (Leviticus 17:11). When the writer of Hebrews explains the Old Testament sacrificial system to his readers he declares that the forgiveness of sins is *impossible* apart from the shedding of blood (Hebrews 9:22).

Consequently, Moses must be praying for the restoration of happiness predicated upon a heart-changing solution to their sins. To grant happiness apart from atonement would be no solution at all; it would be like treating cancer with a band-aid, and would not deal with the problem of sin and the fatal judgment that follows. Moses' request assumes that a decisive atonement will be made. The prophet reaches forward to the certainty that God will be faithful to His covenant and will therefore exercise His *ḥesed* via a sufficient propitiation on behalf of His chosen people.

---

[3] We must keep Romans 9:6 ("they are not all Israel who are descended from Israel") in our hip pocket as we consider these mysteries. There was an external aspect of the Old Covenant that was not matched by internal spiritual realities.

A PRAYER OF MOSES

This is crucial: don't miss it! Moses is asking for the fulfillment of God's covenant promises in verse 14; he's not asking for joy or happiness that is somehow disconnected from the covenant. Such joy in a fallen, rebellious world is impossible apart from a blood-atonement for sin, for you can't have enduring happiness *if you remain the object of God's wrath*. To fail to see this is to miss the point of Psalm 90.

Moses seeks for God's people to be **satisfied**[4] not with bread, but with God's **lovingkindness**. The kingdom of God is the fullest expression of His covenant loving-kindness (Matthew 6:25-33). This is why Jesus Christ in the Sermon on the Mount encourages His listeners not to be anxious for food or clothing but to seek first God's kingdom. Earthly pleasures and treasures are destined for the moth, rust, and corruption (Matthew 6:19-20), but the comforts of our God are forever. When Christ, the "Lamb of God who takes away the sin of the world" (John 1:29), invites us to seek the kingdom and lay up treasures in heaven He reveals Himself as the solution to our sins, and therefore God's final answer to Moses' heartfelt prayer.

Verses 5-6 had presented the **morning** as a time of futility and vain hope because it precedes an evening of withering and death. But verse 14, reflecting the expectation of covenant grace, portrays the morning as a new era of satisfaction in God, a period of joy that

---

4 This verb normally appears in a context of food.

Chapter 10: A Plea for Covenant Lovingkindness (Part 1), v 14

will last **all our days**. In Lamentations 3:22-23 Jeremiah echoes this, affirming that God's lovingkindnesses never cease and are new every morning.[5]

The second half of the line reveals the intent of the plea contained in the first half: the writer desires God's lovingkindness *so that* His people may **cry out with joy**, rejoicing for all of their days. God's lovingkindness is the true source of enduring joy: "Thou wilt make known to me the path of life; In Thy presence is fulness of joy; In Thy right hand there are pleasures forever" (Psalm 16:11).

The first use of this verb ("cry out with joy") occurs in Leviticus 9:24. Aaron and his sons are directed to make an atoning offering for the people (9:7). Aaron first offers sacrifices for himself, thus qualifying him to act in behalf of the people, and then presents a sin offering, a burnt offering, and a peace offering (9:22). He then enters into the Tent of Meeting with Moses. Emerging, he and Moses bless the people and the glory of God appears. In a flash of fire, the sacrifices which have been burning upon the altar are completely consumed, signifying God's acceptance of and pleasure with the offering. The people fall upon their faces with a *shout* of joy (9:24). This larger context presents a great snapshot of the how the verb is employed in the majority of its appearances in the Old Testament.

---

[5] It interesting, too, that both Jeremiah and Moses write in a similar context of judgment.

It shows up repeatedly in Isaiah (14 times), each instance being in the context of holy joy associated with the shout of God's people.[6] It makes many appearances in the Psalms, always in the context of joy and rejoicing. "The frequent employment of the term indicates decisively that the highest mood of OT religion was joy."[7] The accompanying verb ("**and rejoice**") shows that the action ("**cry out with joy**") is expressing the overflow of a powerful emotion ("**rejoice**").

"**All of our days**" takes the reader back, by way of contrast, to the same expression in verse 9. There the miserable days of the guilty sinner decline through God's overflowing fury against sin. But here the plea is for days filled with the joy of God's covenant lovingkindness. There the sinner's days end like a sigh or a whimper; here, because of God's lovingkindness, the redeemed sinner's days are filled with the shout of exultation and the cry of rejoicing. Once again we are compelled to understand this prayer as a bold plea for divine favor based squarely upon God's gracious covenant promises and not upon any merit of the recipients.

As new covenant readers of Psalm 90 who look back upon the cross and the resurrection, we understand that Moses' prayer seeking satisfaction and joy through God's covenant lovingkindness is a prayer that can not be answered apart from *God's divine justice being satisfied through Christ's propitiating sacrifice for sins.*

---

6   William White, in TWOT, 2179.
7   Ibid.

CHAPTER 10: A PLEA FOR COVENANT LOVINGKINDNESS (PART 1), V 14

That which Moses has named as the problem—our sins—must be decisively atoned before we can be accepted. The forgiveness of sins enables us to enjoy Him in all His glorious, radiant holiness without fear of judgment. Enjoying His presence free from guilt will produce overpowering floods of joy and shouts of rejoicing.

On the night before Jesus went to the cross to make the final sacrifice He spoke of the fullness of joy His followers would experience: "These things I have spoken to you, that My joy may be in you, and that your joy may be made full" (John 15:11). Jesus told His disciples that their sorrow over His soon-to-be-accomplished crucifixion would be replaced by great joy when they understood what His sacrifice accomplished: "Therefore you too now have sorrow; but I will see you again, and your heart will rejoice, and no one takes your joy away from you" (John 16:22).

In a fulfillment of Moses' prayer that is "exceeding abundantly beyond all that we ask or think" (Ephesians 3:20), Peter tells us that even in the midst of great trials and suffering, because of Jesus Christ we have "*joy inexpressible*." Does this not fit with the prophet's request that we "rejoice all of our days"?

> In this you greatly rejoice, even though now for a little while, if necessary, you have been distressed by various trials, that the proof of your faith, being more precious than gold which is perishable, even though tested by fire, may be

> found to result in praise and glory and honor at the revelation of Jesus Christ; and though you have not seen Him, you love Him, and though you do not see Him now, but believe in Him, you greatly rejoice with joy inexpressible and full of glory, obtaining as the outcome of your faith the salvation of your souls. (1 Peter 1:6-9)

Peter hammers home the truth that joy is not a product of earthly ease and comfort, but the result of God's faithful covenant lovingkindness expressed through Jesus Christ.

Chapter 10: A Plea for Covenant Lovingkindness (Part 1), v 14

Food for Thought

Read Psalm 90, then focus on verse 14.

1. What is God's lovingkindness and upon what is it based?

2. What lines of evidence can we cite to support the supposition that Moses must be assuming a solution to the problem of sin in his request of verse 14?

3. Contrast the expressions "in the morning" and "all our days" with their appearances in verses 5-6 and 9. What accounts for the difference in tone?

4. What sort of relationship is there between sin and joy? How must the first affect the second?

5. The pleasures of sin are "for a season" (Hebrews 11:25). Contrast that with the latter part of verse 14.

6. How does the presence of sin in your life impact your experience of joy?

Chapter 11: A Plea for Covenant Lovingkindness (Part 2), v 15

15 Cause us to rejoice according to the days you have disciplined us; according to the years we have seen misery.

Verse 15 is formed from a double pair of terse expressions employing both parallelism and ellipsis.[1] Parallelism occurs when the writer restates what he has just said, but using different words either to advance the point or to show contrast, etc. Ellipsis occurs when the writer leaves out words that the reader must supply; it is part of what makes poetry so terse and powerful. For ease of reference I have numbered the expressions 1-4. The text in italics is the elliptical portion that the reader is expected to supply.

> Expression A: Cause us to rejoice
>
> Expression B: according to the days you have disciplined us;
>
> Expression C: *Cause us to rejoice*
>
> Expression D: *according to the* years we have seen misery

Expression C is parallel to expression A. Expression D is parallel to expression B, advancing the thought as will be seen below.

In expression A (and by implication, expression C)

---

[1] Hebrew scholars would call these "expressions" cola (singular: colon), the pairs being "bicola." In order to reduce the technical aspects of this study I have relabeled them "expressions."

A PRAYER OF MOSES

Moses makes a request of divine, sovereign grace: **cause us to rejoice**. Elsewhere in Scripture we find similar pleas or statements regarding God <u>causing</u> human responses. The same verb in the same imperative form appears in Ps 86:4 : "<u>Make glad</u> the soul of Thy servant, For to Thee, O Lord, I lift up my soul." The factor of divine causation brings to mind verses such as 1 Peter 1:3 in which Peter blesses God, who has "<u>caused</u> us to be born again," or James 1:18 where James speaks about the "exercise of His will" by which He "brought us forth by the word of truth." Moses seeks just such a display of divine sovereignty: "cause us to rejoice!"

The only sort of grace that can accomplish this is *sovereign* grace. Why is this so? Clearly it is because of the corrupting power of sin. Consider for instance what David writes in the first three verses of Psalm 14. David says that God looks from heaven to see if there are any who seek after Him. Paul rephrases this in categorical terms: "There is none who seeks for God" (Romans 3:11b).

Meditate on that bombshell for a moment. Seven simple words, but devastating in their impact. Combine them with the words of Jesus in John 6:44, "No one can come to Me unless the Father who sent Me draws him." Sovereign grace is the *sine qua non*, the essential condition necessary for a man to pursue God. God must first pursue us! Moses' request is the theologically astute plea of a man who has watched the people of

God run after idolatry even in the face of jaw-dropping divine miracles. We *need* sovereign grace!

Moses asks for this blessing of rejoicing "**according to the days you have disciplined us**." With the measure God has used to mete out chastening, the prophet desires that God also return joy. Expression D restates the request of expression B in the form, "**the years we have seen misery**." "**Days**" and "**years**" refer to an extended time of chastening and should not be interpreted with some sort of precision. It is likely that Moses is thinking of the general forty-year wandering period of judgment, and he now asks for a season of blessing on the young generation who will be crossing the Jordan not many days hence.[2]

The pattern of blessing following affliction appears in Psalm 30, in which David rejoices over answered prayer after a period of suffering. He makes reference to the gladness of God that follows suffering: "For His anger is but for a moment, His favor is for a lifetime; Weeping may last for the night, But a shout of joy comes in the morning" (Psalm 30:5).

An important distinction exists between expressions B and D (aside from the advance in time reference, "days" to "years") which carries forward the thought. Expression B, "**the days you have disciplined us**," speaks from God's perspective of disciplining an erring

---

2   I am assuming Psalm 90 was written at or near the end of Moses' life. It is heavily scented with a world-weariness that makes this a good guess, though it could have been written earlier.

servant. Expression D, "**the years we have seen misery**," speaks of the same discipline, but from the perspective of the misery of the one so disciplined.

When God afflicts or disciplines (*'anah*) His children He always has a specific purpose standing just behind the veil. In Psalm 119:75, the psalmist (using the same stem of the verb as in 90:15) affirms that afflictions from God arise out of His faithfulness: "I know, O LORD, that Thy judgments are righteous, And that in faithfulness Thou hast <u>afflicted</u> me" (Psalm 119:75).

This is readily observed in Moses' speech in Deuteronomy 8. He uses the same verb (*'anah*, translated above in Ps 90:15 as "disciplined," or "afflicted" in the NASB) in Deuteronomy 8:2, 3, and 16 (the NASB renders it as "humble" or "humbled"). In 8:2 , God "humbled" the children of Israel through the wilderness experience as a test to know "whether you would keep His commandments or not." In 8:3 , God allowed them to hunger, and then fed them supernaturally with manna:

> He humbled you . . . that He might make you understand that man does not live by bread alone, but man lives by everything that proceeds out of the mouth of the LORD.

In verse 16, Moses states that God fed them with manna, "that He might <u>humble</u> you and that He might test you, to do good for you in the end." This purpose, "to do good for you in the end," is remarkably similar

Chapter 11: A Plea for Covenant Lovingkindness (Part 2), v 15

to what Moses seeks in Psalm 90:15: joy and rejoicing which outweigh the days of chastening and misery.[3]

The idea of "suffering now for the purpose of joy later" is modeled by Jesus Himself. According to Hebrews 12:2, Jesus willingly entered into the suffering of the cross for the purpose of the joy that would follow. It is interesting that Hebrews 12 encourages us to continue on in the midst of the misery of discipline, and for the same reason Jesus endured His suffering: because of the yield it produces in terms of the "peaceful fruit of righteousness" (Hebrews 12:11).

The noun "**misery**" is used as a collective to denote the sum of sorrow and misfortune one experiences over a lifetime.[4] The upshot of Moses' plea in verse 15 is that the eventual joy and rejoicing brought about by the favor of the Lord might outweigh the affliction and sorrow He permits as He tests, teaches, and forms us in accord with His will.

Once again we find the abundant answer to Moses' plea in Christ Himself. After telling us that God has given us the knowledge of His glory in the face of Jesus Christ, Paul assures us:

> Therefore we do not lose heart, but though our outer man is decaying, yet our inner man is

---

[3] Texts like Deuteronomy 8 comprise additional reasons for believing that the specific setting of Psalm 90 is at or near the end of the Wilderness wandering and thus at or near the end of Moses' life.

[4] G. Herbert Livingston, in TWOT, article 2191c. It appears over twenty times with this sense.

being renewed day by day. For momentary, light affliction is producing for us an eternal weight of glory far beyond all comparison, while we look not at the things which are seen, but at the things which are not seen; for the things which are seen are temporal, but the things which are not seen are eternal. (2 Corinthians 4:16-18)

Excursus: Should Christians Pursue their own Joy?

In verses 14 and 15 of Psalm 90, Moses appears to sanctify the pursuit of joy as a motive worthy of the believer: "Satisfy us in the morning with your lovingkindness, that *[indicates purpose]* we may cry out with joy and rejoice for all our days. Cause us to rejoice . . ."

Such a notion contrasts sharply with those who claim that true Christian service, in order to be praiseworthy, must be performed without any thought of reward. Somehow we are to respond to God's commands as persons disinterested in our own futures and fortunes, as though God was more glorified that way. Some claim that if we serve because of our own interest we become little more than mercenaries, consequently *we must have a holy indifference to outcomes and rewards, and serve God because it is our duty to do so*. That certainly has the ring of godliness. It promotes the appearance of a well-disciplined Christian life. It sounds quite impressive. But is it what the Bible teaches?

Let's clarify the issue a little by asking a series of questions: does personal pleasure motivate you to do *any-*

CHAPTER 11: A PLEA FOR COVENANT LOVINGKINDNESS (PART 2), V 15

thing? Is the raw experience of joy motivating? Do you enjoy joy? Do you want more?

What if we are pursuing our own joy in Christ? What if we are pursuing our enjoyment of God? What, then, *if we are motivated by our joy in Christ and our enjoyment of God*? Does the fact that we are motivated by our own pleasure pollute that service to Christ which brings us pleasure? Or, conversely, does it add to God's glory by revealing Him as pleasurable and enjoyable? Does not pursuing Christ because He is the source of true joy and pleasure reveal His surpassing worth and inestimable value?

John Piper, in a brief exposition of Philippians 1:20-21, captures this point perfectly. First, let's hear Paul:

> . . . according to my earnest expectation and hope, that I shall not be put to shame in anything, but that with all boldness, Christ shall even now, as always, be exalted in my body, whether by life or by death. For to me, to live is Christ, and to die is gain.

Piper says this:

> The common denominator between living and dying is that Christ is the all-satisfying treasure that we embrace whether we live or die. Christ is praised by being prized. He is magnified as a glorious treasure when He becomes our unrivaled pleasure. So if we are going to praise

Him and magnify Him, we dare not be indifferent as to whether we prize Him and find pleasure in Him. If Christ's honor is our passion, *the pursuit of pleasure in Him is our duty.*[5]

I propose that when we pursue our joy in God we are fulfilling the model of Jesus Christ, Who, *for the joy set before Him* endured the cross (Hebrews 12:2). Once you remove the blinders of a "disinterested altruism" it is amazing to see how often God the Holy Spirit employs the motivation of joy and reward with God's elect. Consider these verses (the emphases are mine):

- Do you not know that those who run in a race all run, but *only one receives the prize? Run in such a way that you may win.* And everyone who competes in the games exercises self-control in all things. *They then do it to receive a perishable wreath, but we an imperishable.* (1 Corinthians 9:24-25)

- Whatever you do, do your work heartily, as for the Lord rather than for men; *knowing that from the Lord you will receive the reward of the inheritance.* It is the Lord Christ whom you serve. (Colossians 3:23-24)

- By faith Moses, when he had grown up, refused to be called the son of Pharaoh's daughter;

---

5 John Piper, *The Dangerous Duty of Delight*, Colorado Springs: Multnomah, 2001, p. 27, emphasis mine. A complete discussion of the notion of pursuing pleasure in Christ can be found in chapters 4-5 of this remarkable little volume.

choosing rather to endure ill-treatment with the people of God, than to enjoy the passing pleasures of sin; considering the reproach of Christ greater riches than the treasures of Egypt; *for he was looking to the reward.* (Hebrews 11:24-26)

- Behold, I am coming quickly, and *My reward is with Me, to render to every man according to what he has done.* (Revelation 22:12)

- I have fought the good fight, I have finished the course, I have kept the faith; *in the future there is laid up for me the crown of righteousness,* which the Lord, the righteous Judge, will award to me on that day; and not only to me, but also to all who have loved His appearing. (2 Timothy 4:7-8)

In fact, I would go further: I suggest that the model of disinterested altruism is plainly *unbiblical*. It places too much weight on the goodness of unglorified human nature and does not place enough weight on the goodness and generosity of God.

C. S. Lewis addresses this notion of the goodness of pursuing our pleasure in Christ in a memorable passage from his sermon, *The Weight of Glory*:

If there lurks in most modern minds the notion that to desire our own good and earnestly to hope for the enjoyment of it is a bad thing, I

> submit that this notion has crept in from Kant and the Stoics and is no part of the Christian faith. Indeed, if we consider the unblushing promises of reward and the staggering nature of the rewards promised in the Gospels, it would seem that Our Lord finds our desires, not too strong, but too weak. We are half-hearted creatures, fooling about with drink and sex and ambition when infinite joy is offered us, like an ignorant child who wants to go on making mud pies in a slum because he cannot imagine what is meant by the offer of a holiday at the sea. We are far too easily pleased.[6]

If one was to allow that perhaps pursuing pleasure in Christ is permissible so long as it is the right sort of pleasure, I would respond, "But of course! We are talking about *regenerate* people, after all, not unregenerate ones!" Only redeemed individuals have experienced the sort of divine heart surgery that redefines our pleasures and loves.

In short, we must indeed see Moses as pursuing joy in Jehovah. He's asking that God's elect servants be satisfied with God's great lovingkindness for the purpose of joy and gladness. May we deluge the throne of God with requests for the same, and for the same reasons!

---

6   Taken from C. S. Lewis, *The Weight of Glory*. Accessed on 6/5/2012 at http://www.verber.com/mark/xian/weight-of-glory.pdf.

CHAPTER 11: A PLEA FOR COVENANT LOVINGKINDNESS (PART 2), V 15

Food for Thought

Read Psalm 90, then focus on verse 15.

1. How is expression A dependent upon sovereign grace? What in the text clues us in to the fact that Moses is specifically asking for *sovereign* grace. [Note: read question 2 below before answering question 1. Note that the two questions are asking two *different* things: "*what*" and "*why*." Be sure to read each carefully.]

2. Why do we need *sovereign* grace?

3. How does expression D advance and add to the thought of expression B?

4. How specifically does Jesus Christ model the principle of suffering now for the purpose of joy later?

5. Should Christians pursue their own joy? Why or why not?

Chapter 12: A Plea for Covenant Fellowship, v 16

16 Let your work appear to your servants, and your splendor unto their sons.

Before we examine more closely what Moses is asking for, let's not miss the striking irony. *Let your work appear to your servants*? Oh, please! Is this request really necessary? How could God's work be any more obvious and visible? Think of how God had already displayed His amazing divine activity on their behalf: the plagues in Egypt, the crossing of the Red Sea on dry ground, the water from rocks, and the daily provision of manna. Not only that, but the glory of His presence was visibly displayed: hovering over the tabernacle in plain sight was the cloud of God's presence by day and the fire by night. How could they possibly *miss* such obvious manifestations of God's work? And yet . . . .

Some years ago, I was privileged to serve on the administrative staff of Westminster Theological Seminary in Philadelphia. I was attending the school in pursuit of training that would sharpen my skills as a pastor, and God graciously provided employment for me on campus as a computer support person. A year later I was invited to serve as the school's Information Technology director. It was a great opportunity, and one of the benefits of the position was that I could attend classes tuition free.

After graduation I remained on staff while I began sending out resumes to re-enter ministry, or to land a teaching position in a Bible college. Several opportunities arose, only to have the doors repeatedly slam shut at the last moment. After months without success I became frustrated and discontent, and felt as if God was not providing opportunities to serve Him. My sinful attitude spilled over into my work, to the point that one day I angrily exploded at my supervisor. When I saw the shock and hurt written in her face the Holy Spirit of God brought me up short, humbling me and showing my discontent for precisely what it was: sinful faithlessness and ingratitude.

What had happened? Despite God's wonderful provision for my family and me throughout my seminary years, despite the fact that I had been able to complete my seminary degree tuition free, *I had lost sight of the works of God*. I shouldn't have, but I did. God's gracious deeds on my behalf were clear, obvious, and amazing. *How could I have missed them?*

By the grace of God, I confessed my sin and sought forgiveness from the Lord and from my supervisor. I began to view my work at Westminster as I should have all along: as an opportunity to serve and minister to my co-workers in the name of Christ.

My own experience tells me that Moses' request in verse 16 is more apropos than is immediately apparent, and herein is one of the benefits of the psalms. They are not bound to specific situations in life. This is intentional since they are vehicles of worship, prayer, complaint,

Chapter 12: A Plea for Covenant Fellowship, v 16

confession, and so on, for *all* time. Because they are not specific to a given situation we may read them, pray them, and apply them to our own context in life.

With this thought in mind, let's take a closer look at what Moses says here. Verse 16 is another sample of elliptical synonymous parallelism.[1] The brevity achieved through ellipsis is part of what enables poetry to punch far above its weight. The ellipsis expanded is, "Let your work appear . . . , and *let* your splendor *appear* . . . ." The verse contains two expanding parallel thrusts: "your work" advances to "your splendor," and "your servants" moves forward to "their sons."

"**Work**" is the translation of a noun (*po'al*) which, when used to refer to God's deeds, normally points to His deeds in *history* rather than *creation*.[2] Moses desires that the chosen people would be able to trace God's hand in their history and that the clear vision of the past would result in faith—and faithfulness—for the present.

But the thought is not only that the current generation of Israelites in the wilderness would keep in mind what God has already done, as important as that is. Moses is also praying that God's glorious works on behalf of His covenant people *continue* apace. Put another way,

---

[1] For a description of the terms "elliptical" and "parallelism" see the first page of chapter 11. "Synonymous" refers to the category of parallelism in Hebrew poetry in which the writer advances the thought in nearly the same terms.
[2] Victor P. Hamilton, in TWOT, article 1792a.

A PRAYER OF MOSES

Moses desires that the future generations of readers of the psalm ("**their sons**") continue to see God's wonderful works ("**let your work appear**") in their own future time. The thought is appropriate for a psalm whose concerns span "from everlasting to everlasting" (v. 2).

Thus this is a prayer for currency. It is a prayer that God would *continue* to do His amazing deeds in the future life of His covenant people. It's a good prayer for the church today. Leupold says,

> But for a servant of God to be unaware of what God is doing and not to see at least some dim glimpses of the success of God's work can well be the cause of utter hopelessness.[3]

Any congregation (or individual believer) whose primary testimonies consist of what God did twenty and thirty years ago should to drop to their knees and seek God's face, as Moses did, with this prayer on their lips until they become aware of what God is doing at present. God is at work right now through His mighty Son! Paul reminds us that the many promises of God are all "*YES*" in Christ Jesus (2 Corinthians 1:20).

"**Let your work appear to your servants**" is also a prayer of disclosure. Moses prays that God would disclose Himself and His deeds; remember Exodus 33:18, "Show me your glory!" The apostle John responds, "we beheld His glory" (John 1:14)!

---
3 Leupold, 648.

In fact, it almost appears that John wrote his gospel with half an eye on Psalm 90. In John's gospel Jesus says that He (or the Holy Spirit whom He would send) discloses to His followers the Father's works:

- 15:15 "All things that I have heard from my Father I have made known to you"

- 15:26 "When the Helper comes . . . , He will testify about Me"

- 16:13 "He will guide you into all the truth . . . , He will disclose what is to come"

- 16:14 "He will take of mine and disclose it to you"

- 17:6 "I have manifested Your Name to the men You gave Me"

- 17:8 "the words You gave Me, I have given them"

Near the end of John's gospel, the apostle writes:

> Many other signs therefore Jesus also performed in the presence of the disciples, which are not written in this book; but these have been written that you may believe that Jesus is the Christ, the Son of God; and that believing you may have life in His name. (John 20:30-31)

God's work appears fully in the work of Jesus Christ.

The second expression of verse 16 expands on the first: **"And your splendor unto their sons."** The word translated "splendor" appears several times in the psalms, often rendered as "majesty." For instance, Psalm 29:4 says that the voice of the Lord is "majestic." Sometimes the word is translated as "majesty" and appears in combination with a *different* word that is rendered as "splendor," such as Psalm 96:6, "Splendor and majesty are before Him." In Psalm 104:1, God is "clothed with splendor and majesty." In Psalm 111:3, God's work is "splendid and majestic." Psalm 145 echoes some of the same themes contained in this last section of Moses' psalm: "On the glorious splendor[4] of thy majesty, and on thy wonderful works I will meditate" (Psalm 145:6).

In the parallelism of verse 16, "splendor" pushes the thought of God's works forward, going beyond the idea of God's *deeds* to the glorious effulgence of His *presence*. It is likely that Moses has in mind the *shekinah* glory that dwelt in the most holy place of the tabernacle (also referred to as the "tent of meeting"). When Moses had finished erecting the newly constructed tabernacle, the splendor and glory of God's presence filled it:

> And he erected the court all around the tabernacle and the altar, and hung up the veil for the gateway of the court. Thus Moses finished the work. Then the cloud covered the tent of meeting, and the glory of the LORD filled the

---

[4] Hebrew: "splendor of glory."

tabernacle. And Moses was not able to enter the tent of meeting because the cloud had settled on it, and the glory of the LORD filled the tabernacle. (Exodus 40:33-35)

The apostle John makes clear that Jesus is God in the flesh, displaying the very glory of God: "And the Word became flesh, and dwelt [lit: *tabernacling*] among us, and *we beheld His glory*, glory as of the only begotten from the Father, full of grace and truth" (John 1:14, emphasis mine). The writer of Hebrews expands on this truth, telling us that while God in the past has spoken through the prophets, He has now spoken "in His Son" (Hebrews 1:1-2). The Greek text says, literally, "in Son," referring to the fact that the *mode* of revelation has advanced from the papyrus scrolls of the prophets to flesh of God incarnate. Notice that the writer of Hebrews says that Jesus "is the *radiance of His glory*:"

> God, after He spoke long ago to the fathers in the prophets in many portions and in many ways, in these last days has spoken to us in His Son, whom He appointed heir of all things, through whom also He made the world. And He is the radiance of His glory and the exact representation of His nature, and upholds all things by the word of His power. When He had made purification of sins, He sat down at the right hand of the Majesty on high . . . (Hebrews 1:1-3)

A Prayer of Moses

Again and again, the careful reader of this beautiful psalm is struck by the precise manner in which Jesus Christ is the divine fulfillment of the longings of Moses' heart. In the days of Jesus' earthly ministry, He performed the works of the Father in a way designed to be a visible signpost, a witness, that He was sent by the Father:

> But the witness which I have is greater than that of John; for the works which the Father has given Me to accomplish, the very works that I do, bear witness of Me, that the Father has sent Me. (John 5:36)

In the context of this statement, Jesus says, "For if you believed Moses, you would believe Me; *for he wrote of Me*" (John 5:46, emphasis mine).

God's work and His splendor *has* appeared to His servants, just as Moses asked. Jesus Christ is God's final revelation of Himself, doing the work of God and displaying His splendor as the unique Son of God. The New Testament stands for all time as the record of God's glorious revelation in Christ, so that not only did the Father's works and splendor "appear to your servants," but also "to their children," the many generations that have followed. The New Testament explains to us the very nature of Jesus Christ, His work on the cross, and the many blessings He has secured for those who place their trust in Him. Truly, all the promises of God are "*YES!*" in Jesus Christ.

CHAPTER 12: A PLEA FOR COVENANT FELLOWSHIP, V 16

Food for Thought

Read Psalm 90, then focus on verse 16.

1. Why might the expression "let your work appear to your servants" seem to be so ironic a request?

2. On the other hand, why is that expression not as ironic as might appear?

3. How is verse 16 a "prayer for currency?" What does that mean?

4. What are some ways in which you have seen God's work in your own life in the last three months? Be specific.

5. Explain how the reality of Christ answers to the request of Moses.

Chapter 13: God the Gracious Sustainer, v 17

17 May the delight of the Lord our God be upon us, and establish the work of our hands upon us, indeed, the work of our hands, establish it.

I love cartoons. I'm not talking about the Saturday morning stuff. No, I'm talking about the wonderful animated feature films that are ostensibly produced for kids, but are truly understood only by adults. One of my favorites is Disney's Pixar creation, *The Incredibles*. It's a film about the Parr family, who on first appearance seem to be an average suburban family, but are actually super-heroes traveling incognito. They've been forced underground by a society who seem set on litigating their benefactors out of existence.

The film opens before the legal climate has become so hostile. A series of super-hero interviews sets the stage for what is to follow. Red-suited Mr. Incredible (who becomes meek and mild-mannered Bob Parr when later forced underground) makes this comment during his interview:

> No matter how many times you save the world, it always manages to get back in jeopardy again. *Sometimes I just want it to stay saved*! You know, for a little bit? I feel like the maid; I just cleaned up this mess! Can we keep it clean for . . . for ten minutes![1]

---
1 http://www.imdb.com/title/tt0317705/quotes. Accessed on 11/14/2012

This is effectively what Moses is asking for in the final verse of Psalm 90. It reflects an experience every believer has had: you think you've nailed down an area of your life, so you turn to work on a different area and before you know it the previous problem has reappeared. We long for the "work of our hands" to be "established;" we want our world to "*stay saved*!"

Moses' final petition asks for God's delight to be upon His people. The noun "**delight**" is translated variously "beauty," "pleasantness," "kindness," "favor" and in some translations, "graciousness." Using the same word, David says in Psalm 27:4:

> One thing I have asked from the LORD, that I shall seek: That I may dwell in the house of the LORD all the days of my life, To behold the beauty of the LORD, And to meditate in His temple.

So what exactly is Moses desiring? Is he perhaps requesting that God's people bear His image ("May the *beauty* of the Lord our God *be upon us*")? Or is it a request for God's grace ("May the *favor* . . . "), or God's goodness in the land ("May the *pleasantness* . . . ")? There is some ambiguity here.

If we read the verse in the light of poetic parallelism we see that Moses relates God's delight to the establishment of the works of His servants' hands.[2] We are inten-

---

[2] The repetition of *'ālênū*, "upon us," strengthens the supposition of parallelism.

ded to see that God's favor is necessary if our efforts are to have enduring success.

A similar idea is found in Moses' third address to the nation, dealing with the terms of the covenant. Moses describes to the people God's blessings (an evidence of His delight) if they will obey Him:

> Then the LORD your God will prosper you abundantly in all the work of your hand, in the offspring of your body and in the offspring of your cattle and in the produce of your ground, for the LORD will again rejoice over you for good, just as He rejoiced over your fathers; if you obey the LORD your God to keep His commandments and His statutes which are written in this book of the law, if you turn to the LORD your God with all your heart and soul. (Deuteronomy 30:9-10)[3]

If this understanding is correct, that God's delight is the necessary condition for the establishment of our works, then Moses' prayer in Psalm 90 *must anticipate covenant obedience on the part of God's servants*, for nothing less is required to establish God's blessings. This anticipated obedience is reflected in the term Moses selects to address God. As he did back in verse 1, Moses addresses God as *'Adonay 'ĕlōhênū*: **"the Lord our**

---

[3] In the context of this passage, Moses first prophesies that the children of Israel will rebelliously default on their covenant obligations. The named blessings are predicated on a return to obedience, but the lesson is the same: God's delight rests upon those who obey Him.

God." Adonai is used frequently as a respectful term to address one of superior authority, and means lord, master, or owner. It is used of husbands, kings, masters of slaves, etc. In the plural form with the first person common singular suffix, as it appears here, it always refers to God and accentuates His sovereign authority and Lordship.[4] By the use of the term Moses reminds the reader that he lives in a covenant relationship with God, a relationship that presupposes obedience to our Adonai, our Master.

Moses completes his supplication with a twice-repeated request that God **establish** the work of His servants. The desire is that the sovereign Master, who is God from everlasting to everlasting (v 2), would fix in permanence the efforts of His people to serve Him. "**Work**" is singular, suggesting that more than individual deeds are indicated (though they would certainly be included in the idea). "**Our hands**" is a poetic way of referring to full product of one's life. In modern terms, Moses is asking for the permanent, successful accomplishment of Israel's "mission statement."

Here is what the reader must see, or he misses the thrust of the psalm: Moses' request for permanence stands in bold contrast to the *temporary, transitory quality of human life expressed in the first two-thirds of the psalm*. The repetition of the request makes it emphatic: "establish the work of our hands . . . indeed, the work of our

---

[4] Robert L. Alden, in TWOT, article 27b.

hands, establish it." This request is the ultimate point of Moses' prayer.

There are at least five significant observations we can carry away from Psalm 90:17. First, for Moses there are both personal and national implications to his prayer. Moses knows that he himself will not be allowed to enter the Promised Land and is about to die (Numbers 27:12-14). He desires that his own life-work of shepherding God's people, leading them out of Egypt, handing over to them the book of the Law, and leading them up to the point of entering the Promised Land will have ultimate, enduring success. God answered his prayer; Israel did enter, conquer and occupy the land as a sovereign state for the next eight hundred years.

Second, beyond their possession of Canaan, the life and times of the Hebrew nation provided the soil in which the fulness of time eventually bloomed resulting in the incarnation of their final and permanent King, their Messiah, Jesus Christ the Son of David. Many scholars have noted that Moses serves as a type of the Redeemer who was to come, and the exodus is portrayed as a type of the final redemption Jesus would bring. As a consequence of the enduring "work of his hands" then, Moses remains the greatest personage in Israel's history, short of Jesus Himself.

But third, examining the data from a different perspective—that of the perfect holiness that God righteously requires of His people—I suppose we could say that this is the place at which Moses' prayer *fails* in terms of anticipated covenant obedience. The history of God's people from beginning to end demonstrates conclusively that neither Israel nor the Church (nor you nor I) have ever exercised the covenant obedience necessary under the Mosaic arrangement. On our part it is an unremitting, unbroken record of failure. From this perspective the Mosaic Law establishes something, but it isn't our redemption. It is our condemnation. Paul says quite clearly:

> Now we know that whatever the Law says, it speaks to those who are under the Law, that every mouth may be closed, and all the world may become accountable to God; because by the works of the Law no flesh will be justified in His sight; for through the Law comes the knowledge of sin. (Romans 3:19-20)

Beyond that, because of the taint of transgression the works of our hands *shouldn't be established* since they are polluted with sins such as pride, mixed motives, and even rebellion against the everlasting God. It is the wrath—not the delight—of the Master that rests upon such works and the workers who perpetrate them.

But there is a fourth point that carries the day and turns Moses' prayer into an overwhelming blessing. Because of God's great love and mercy and His compassions which never fail, even when we were dead in our trespasses and sins, our great God made us alive together in

Christ. Herein is Jesus—alone—truly the answer to the prayer of Moses. Jesus Christ is the model Hebrew, the representative Israelite, the last Adam who alone gave to the Father complete and unqualified covenant obedience. Jesus claimed in John 8:29, " . . . I always do the things that are pleasing to Him." Only in Christ is the Law of Moses finally fulfilled in blazing perfect righteousness. And miracle of all miracles, grace of all grace, it is *this* perfect righteousness that has been credited to those who are in Christ (2 Corinthians 5:21) through repentance and faith in His saving work on the cross. Moses' prayer is answered by the vast delight and pleasure that God has in His wholly obedient Son and, by extension through our union with Him, the delight He has in each of us who have been redeemed through faith in Christ.

And there is a fifth point. If it is true that the delight of the Lord our God is now upon us through Christ then we would expect to see the corollary as well: the works of our hands will be established. This indeed we do see. Jesus Christ Himself explicitly guarantees the fulfillment of this portion of the prayer of Moses in at least two places. First, He promises His disciples, " . . . I will build My church; and the gates of Hades shall not overpower it" (Matthew 16:18). Second, Jesus says in John 15:16:

> You did not choose Me, but I chose you, and appointed you, that you should go and bear fruit, and that *your fruit should remain*, that whatever

you ask of the Father in My name, He may give to you. (emphasis mine)

As Paul exhorts us in 1 Corinthians 15:58:

Therefore, my beloved brethren, be steadfast, immovable, always abounding in the work of the Lord, *knowing that your toil is not in vain in the Lord.* (emphasis mine)

Food for Thought

Read Psalm 90, then focus on verse 17.

1. What does Moses mean when he asks that God's "delight . . . be upon us"?

2. For what is Moses asking when he seeks "the work of our hands" to be established?

3. What are you doing with your life that will endure for eternity?

4. How can God's delight be upon someone when they fail to maintain the covenant obedience that the Law requires?

5. Is God's delight upon you? List at least three things that support your answer.

Chapter 14: Jesus Christ, the Victor over Death!

What an amazing psalm this is, this prayer of Moses the man of God! And how completely God has answered Moses' plea through the work of His Son Jesus Christ!

We began this study with the contemplation of death. Moses' psalm forces us to look seriously at the brevity of life caused by God's righteous wrath that burns against our sins. Moses' own life experiences gave him a unique backdrop against which to paint God's anger.

But we also saw that Moses boldly prays for God's mercy, compassion, and grace. He has no grounds on which to make these requests other than God's gracious nature and covenant promises. Moses moves far beyond a paltry prayer of mere relief; he asks for life-long joy!

Over and over again as we have studied this psalm, we have seen how Jesus Christ alone is the answer to the prayer of Moses. And He is not a *merely sufficient* answer, either, but the abundant, overflowing, beyond-all-we-ask-or-think answer. Given our sin and rebellion we dared not hope for such grace, but God has provided it freely and abundantly through Christ.

Let's review how Jesus is the solution to our sins, to God's wrath, and to the brevity of life. God has shown us that we are sinners (Isaiah 64:6, Romans 3:10, 23). He has also declared that there is but one eternal penalty for sin: death (Ezekiel 18:3; Romans 6:23). He made it clear that though vast unnumbered multitudes walk this broad road of destruction, the penalty will be executed (Matthew 7:13-14); there's no hiding out in the common human idea that, "well, He can't punish everybody!" Yes, He can.

Our situation, in fact, is such that we frankly have no hope (Ephesians 2:12) unless God Himself initiates a rescue. Into this picture of despair steps Jesus Christ, God the Son clothed in human flesh. He lived a righteous life (he "knew no sin," 2 Corinthians 5:21), fulfilling the Law to perfection (Christ is the "end of the Law to everyone who believes," Romans 10:4).

Having lived a completely obedient life such that He merited His Father's favor by virtue of His perfect righteousness, He then willingly bears our transgressions on the cross (1 Peter 2:24), taking upon Himself the wrath of God that was directed against our sins (Isaiah 53:4-6). In the words of 18th century hymn-writer and pastor Robert Robinson, "He, to rescue me from danger, interposed His precious blood . . . ."[1] Jesus Christ placed Himself between us and the righteous wrath of His Father, absorbing the judgment due us in His own body.

His sacrificial death was as perfect and complete as His obedient life had been (Hebrews 10:14-18). God was fully satisfied that the sins placed upon His Son, the sacrificial Lamb of God (John 1:29), were completely

---

[1] Robert Robinson, "Come, Thou Fount of Every Blessing" (Public Domain), v 3.

Chapter 14: Jesus Christ, the Victor over Death!

paid for according to the strictest interpretation of the Law. God's wrath against us was satisfied (or "propitiated," Romans 3:25, 1 John 2:2). Therefore, God raised His Son from the dead (Romans 1:4) as there was no longer any reason for Him to remain in the realm of death. The debt had been paid, reconciliation had been accomplished, the penalty overcome.

For all who place their trust in Jesus Christ as their sole sacrifice for sins, bowing to His sovereign Lordship, God reckons their faith in Christ as righteousness (Romans 3:26; 4:3-5, Galatians 2:16; 3:10-14; 2 Corinthians 5:21). He grants to them all that Jesus accomplished both in His obedient life and sacrificial death.

This is amazing but it gets better still! Just as Christ was raised from the dead we also, who have placed our faith in Him, shall be raised! The entire chapter of 1 Corinthians 15 is dedicated to a defense of the resurrection of Jesus Christ, but Paul extends the argument further to assure us that because Christ was raised so shall we be! He makes the same argument in 1 Thessalonians 4:13-18. Because of Christ we will live forever with joy in the presence and the delight of our heavenly Father. No longer do we need fear the brevity of this life. The writer of Hebrews puts it this way:

> Since then the children share in flesh and blood, He Himself likewise also partook of the same, that through death He might render powerless him who had the power of death, that is, the

devil; and *might deliver those who through fear of death were subject to slavery all their lives.* (Hebrews 2:14-15, emphasis mine)

Jesus Christ is God's perfect fulfillment of the prayer of Moses and God's all-sufficient answer to mankind's deepest needs:

- Did Moses admit that we are sinners? Christ paid for our sins!

- Did Moses lament God's wrath? Christ took upon Himself the wrath due us!

- Did Moses cry out about the condemnation of death? Christ has reversed it for His people!

- Did Moses complain of the brevity of human life? Christ is the victor over death and has guaranteed our resurrection and eternal life by His own resurrection!

- Did Moses ask for wisdom? Christ is to us the wisdom of God!

- Did Moses ask for enduring joy? Christ grants to us abundant joy and rejoicing!

- Did Moses seek God's favor? Christ is the favor of God poured out upon us!

- Did Moses seek for our works to be established? Christ has chosen us to bear fruit—fruit that remains!

So what are our final lessons from Psalm 90? Here are a few thoughts we should take away from this study:

- God dwells in timeless eternity; man is bounded by time and his life is very short.

- Man's disobedience calls forth God's overflowing wrath, by which he is swept away.

- Man is invited to develop a proper perspective of his brevity of life, that through fear of God he may gain a wise heart.

- Man's only hope of enduring permanence is found in covenant obedience and this covenant obedience may only be obtained through faith in the work of Jesus Christ. Only through Christ will the toil of our lives gain enduring significance.

- Where once there was wrath and misery, in Christ we find God's favor and great joy.

Why is Psalm 90 in the Bible? Let me assure you, the purpose of Psalm 90 is not to give you interesting facts about Moses and biblical history. Psalm 90 is in God's Holy Word because He intends to use it to transform *your* life. This is the endgame of the prayer of Moses: the Lord is reminding *you* that *your* life is short and that God's wrath burns hot against *your* sin. God wants *you* to number *your* days and to gain a heart of wisdom and everlasting joy through faith in Christ.

Are you in a covenant relationship with the Lord God through faith in Jesus Christ? Is the favor and delight of God upon you through Christ?

Food for Thought

Read Psalm 90 carefully.

1. List all the ways that Jesus Christ is the perfect and complete answer to Moses' prayer. Be specific; connect specific expressions in Psalm 90 to specific aspects of Jesus Christ's life and ministry.

2. What was Moses' view of the length of human life? Read 1 Corinthians 15:35-57. How does the resurrection impact Moses' lament in Psalm 90?

3. Some people are living in Psalm 90:3-11. Others are living 1 Corinthians 15:58. What determines the difference?

4. What about you? What characterizes you: the terrifying brevity of life, or the overwhelming joy of the resurrection?

Appendix: Verse 3—An Announcement of Death or a Call to Repentance? Or Both?

I want to suggest that verse 3 might be an *intentional double entendre*, based upon four lines of evidence:

1. The semantic range of the verb, "return"
2. The word Moses uses for "dust", and its semantic range
3. The literary structure of the psalm itself
4. The support of context

But first let's consider exactly what the term "double entendre" signifies.

A double entendre is a figure of speech which can convey double meaning. The primary (or obvious) meaning is the one which the audience will grasp most readily. The secondary meaning often requires additional knowledge in order to detect it, such as knowing the semantic domain, or *range of meanings*, belonging to one or more of the words in the expression.

> "Double entendres tend to rely more on multiple meanings of words, or different interpretations of the same primary meaning; they often exploit ambiguity and may be used to introduce it deliberately in a text."[1]

---
1 http://en.wikipedia.org/wiki/Double_entendre (accessed on July 20, 2011).

Sometimes the primary meaning is the only one the author intends; some double entendres are quite unintentional and often very humorous. At other times the double meaning is intentional for the sake of humor, or making a sharp point, or expressing an indelicate notion in inoffensive terms. Puns are a type of a double entendre, and double entendre is sometimes used in poetry.

In modern culture many double entendres are of a sexual nature, often employed in crude humor. But others are very sophisticated, presenting additional levels of meaning beyond the obvious. A fun study of clean double entendre can be found in the many excellent Disney and Pixar animated children's movies.[2] Any adult who has watched them has enjoyed the multilayered sophisticated humor that flies right over the top of their children's heads.

Examine the statements below, and see if you can catch the double meanings:[3]

- Police authorities are finding the solution of murders more and more difficult because the victims are unwilling to cooperate with the police.[4]

---

[2] At the end of *The Incredibles* a new arch-villain is introduced. A groundhog-like figure emerges from the ground riding a massive tunnel-boring device, and in a delightful double entendre he says, "I am the Under-miner! I am always beneath you, *but nothing is beneath me!*"

[3] These examples were copied from http://www.writers-block-help.com/double-entendres.html (accessed on July 20, 2011).

[4] The double meaning is in the word *victims*, which can refer to the ones killed,

APPENDIX: VERSE 3—AN ANNOUNCEMENT OF DEATH OR A CALL TO REPENTANCE? OR BOTH?

- Church Announcement: What is hell? Come to church next Sunday and listen to our new minister![5]

- The ladies of the Walnut Street Mission have discarded clothes. They invite you to come and inspect them.[6]

The Bible employs double entendre. For instance, "You are Peter, and upon this rock I will build my church" (Matthew 16:18). Or Ehud's statement to Eglon in Judges 3:19, "I have a secret message for you, O king." The Hebrew word translated "message" can also be translated "matter" or "thing." Did Ehud have secret words for the king (the primary meaning, which is how Eglon understood him) or did Ehud refer to a secret *thing*, meaning the hidden dagger with which he was about to kill Eglon?[7]

The Song of Solomon is chock full of double entendre: the poem may be read by young people who have no sexual experience, as a pastoral love poem. For sexually-experienced individuals, on the other hand, the Song of Solomon is rather steamy with sexual double entendres that explore the good and holy joy of a marriage relationship.

---

    or to the family members of those killed. Dead people *can't* cooperate with a police investigation!
5 Is the preacher going to preach on hell? Or is listening to him likened to being in hell?
6 Excuse me, but *what* are we inspecting?
7 James D. G. Dunn and John W. Rogerson, eds., *Eerdmans Commentary on the Bible* (Grand Rapids: Eerdmans Publishing Co., 2003) 191.

A Prayer of Moses

Psalm 90:3 says this: *"You cause men to return to dust, saying, 'Return, sons of man!'"* Is this an announcement of death or a call to repentance? Or both? The primary meaning and perhaps the *only* proper meaning of this text is that Moses affirms that it is God who executes judgment upon men. Whatever else may be going on here, this is an announcement of death. We could walk away from the text with only this meaning in mind and have completed our study.

But if there is a dual meaning for this text the secondary meaning would be, *"You cause men to return to contrition, saying, 'Repent, sons of men.'"* What evidence is there for this intriguing possibility?

1. The geographical notion of repentance, and the semantic range of the verb, "return"

The verb translated "return" in Psalm 90:3 (*shuv*) is used in the Old Testament both in a spatial sense (to "turn" away from or towards something, or "return" to a location) and in a metaphoric or spiritual sense (to "turn" or "return" to a condition or to the Lord, hence, to change the mind, relent, or repent). In some texts the spatial idea of turning or returning is so closely linked to the spiritual sense of repentance that the distinction between the two ideas is all but lost. I loosely refer to this phenomenom as *the geographical notion of repentance*, expressing the idea that a change in attitude toward God is always paired with a change of orientation or location with respect to Him. While the

APPENDIX: VERSE 3—AN ANNOUNCEMENT OF DEATH OR A CALL TO REPENTANCE? OR BOTH?

verb *shuv* is often used in texts where this notion is presented, sometimes it is not, demonstrating that the concept does not hang upon a specific word. Four texts provide an adequate sample of the geographical notion of repentance (or its converse, the development of a rebellious heart):

- Genesis 3 contains several instances: after their sin Adam and Eve sew fig leaves to hide their bodies (v. 7) and thus create a barrier expressing a change in orientation; in verse 8, they hide themselves, creating separation through location; and in verse 24 they were driven out of the garden, a change of location God enforces reflecting their spiritual separation from Him.[8]

- Jonah flees "from the presence of the LORD" (Jonah 1:3, a change of location) as an expression of his refusal to obey the command to preach to the Ninevites. He not only leaves the Promised Land as an example of his low spiritual condition, but by the hand of God (1:17, "the LORD appointed a great fish") is separated even further (from the sphere of man's normal habitation, dry land) by being swallowed by the great fish and taken into the deep. He is not returned to dry land until he repents, a change of attitude that results in yet another change of location.

---

8 The verb *shuv* occurs only in verse 19, and there, with its context it simply means to return to the condition of being dust.

- Jesus' parable of the prodigal in Luke 15 illustrates the concept explicitly. The son wickedly demands his portion of the inheritance and upon receiving it immediately goes into a distant country (15:13). The hearers of this parable will recognize that the trip to a "distant country" reveals to the young man's spiritual condition: his heart is far from his father. When he comes to his senses (15:17), his response is to return home (15:18, 20). In other words, his attitude of repentance is manifested by a change of location, just like his earlier rebellion was manifested the same way.

- In the New Testament, Paul uses the terms "far off" and "near" to describe the "before and after" change God effects in the sinner through the blood of Christ (Ephesians 2:13, see also verse 17 which is a free quotation of Isaiah 57:19). In verse 14 he expresses it in terms of the breaking down of barriers.

Notice that it is not always the sinner who effects the change of location; in Genesis 3 it was God who enforced the separation, driving them out of the garden. Jonah experiences God driving him into the deep, away from man's customary habitation.

In the captivities of both the Northern Kingdom (at the hands of Assyrians) and the Southern Kingdom (at the hands of Babylonians), it was God Himself who cast

APPENDIX: VERSE 3—AN ANNOUNCEMENT OF DEATH OR A CALL TO REPENTANCE? OR BOTH?

His people out of the land. Israel and Judah found themselves outside of the Promised Land, captives in far-off place, as a reflection of their own spiritual condition.

It is unsurprizing that God through the prophets *associates the idea of turning or returning with the idea of repentance.* The words underlined below are translated from the same verb used in Ps 90:3, "**return**" (שׁוּב, *shuv*).

- "I have wiped out your transgressions like a thick cloud,And your sins like a heavy mist. Return to Me, for I have redeemed you." (Isaiah 44:22)

- "If you will return, O Israel," declares the LORD, "Then you should return to Me. And if you will put away your detested things from My presence, And will not waver, And you will swear, 'As the LORD lives,' In truth, in justice, and in righteousness; Then the nations will bless themselves in Him, And in Him they will glory." (Jeremiah 4:1-2)

- "And I will give them a heart to know Me, for I am the LORD; and they will be My people, and I will be their God, for they will return to Me with their whole heart." (Jeremiah 24:7)

- "Yet even now," declares the LORD, "Return to Me with all your heart, And with fasting, weeping, and mourning; And rend your heart and not your garments." Now <u>return</u> to the LORD your God, For He is gracious and compassionate, Slow to anger, abounding in lovingkindness, And relenting of evil. Who knows whether He will not <u>turn</u> and relent, And leave a blessing behind Him, Even a grain offering and a libation For the LORD your God? (Joel 2:12-14)

- "Therefore say to them, 'Thus says the LORD of hosts, "<u>Return</u> to Me," declares the LORD of hosts, "that I may <u>return</u> to you," says the LORD of hosts." (Zechariah 1:3)

- "From the days of your fathers you have turned aside from My statutes, and have not kept them. <u>Return</u> to Me, and I will <u>return</u> to you," says the LORD of hosts. "But you say, 'How shall we <u>return</u>?'" (Malachi 3:7)

The same principle can be found in the English language in the expression "turn or burn" in which one is warned to repent ("turn" from their sins and to God—thus repenting by effecting a change of orientation) or face God's judgment. Crass though the expression may be, those simple three words express the gist of an overwhelming number of biblical texts.

So if Moses is using a double entendre he would be presenting God as calling on men to repent in the second half of the verse.

2. The word Moses uses for "dust", and its semantic range

Moses chooses a word for *dust* that we would not expect if he is making a simple reference to Genesis 3:19. It is not עָפָר (*'aphar*) of Genesis 3:19,[9] but is דַּכָּא (*dakka'*) which denotes dust by referencing "that which is crushed" (the verb form, דָּכָא means "to crush"). Perhaps Moses chose as he did in order to contrast God's sovereign power with man's weakness: the Creator is able to effortlessly crush the creature into dust!

Or perhaps Moses chose this term because it can be understood in a way that the word used in Genesis 3:19 can not: it can speak of an attitude of repentance and contrition. For example, the related adjective can be found in Psalm 34:18 (v 19, MT): "The LORD is near to the brokenhearted, And saves those who are crushed in spirit."[10] Note that this verse places in parallel *brokenhearted* and *crushed*. Similarly, Isaiah 57:15 says, "For thus says the high and exalted One Who lives forever, whose name is Holy, 'I dwell on a high and holy place, And also with the contrite [*dakka'*] and lowly of spirit In order to revive the spirit of the lowly And to revive the heart of the contrite [*dakka'*].'"

---

[9] "By the sweat of your face You shall eat bread, Till you return to the ground, Because from it you were taken; For you are dust, And to dust you shall return."

[10] The NASB includes a marginal note offering "contrite" as an alternative to "crushed."

Perhaps Moses is introducing a little intentional ambiguity so that we scratch our heads and consider more carefully what he has said. Maybe he is calling on man in the first half of the verse to return to a broken and contrite heart.

3. The literary structure of the psalm itself

Also supporting the possibility that Moses is referring to repentance or contrition is the structure of the Psalm. Verse 3 as a call to repentance has a balancing bookend in verse 13, such that the two function as an inclusio. Verse 13 may operate as an ironic reversal: in verse 3 God is saying to man "Return!" in the sense of "repent, because death is coming!" In verse 13 man (Moses) is saying to God "Return!" in the sense of "please repent, please change Your mind about all the judgment you have unleashed; remember your covenant!" The irony of these matching bookends would be wholly lost if Moses is simply making reference in verse 3 to man dying.

4. The support of context

On first glance the contextual support for viewing verse 3 as an unambiguous statement about death ("return to dust") is so strong that to look for any additional sense seems as if we are reading meaning into, not out of, the text. Verses 4-10 make a very tight contextual fit tempting us to settle on the notion of death in verse 3. In this interpretation verses 4-10 are presented as the *result* of God's death-dealing wrath. Make no mistake: this is

APPENDIX: VERSE 3—AN ANNOUNCEMENT OF DEATH OR A CALL TO REPENTANCE? OR BOTH?

clearly the primary meaning of verse 3.

And yet the context of the psalm can also be understood as supporting an interpretation of verse 3 as a call for repentance ("Repent, sons of men!"). In this secondary meaning verses 4-10 would be the *reasons given* for the call to repent, "Repent, for life is brief and death is coming!"

A cautionary conclusion

A word means only one thing in a given context regardless of how wide its semantic range may be. Consequently, שׁוּב (*shuv*) in verse 3 means either "return to dust" or "repent" but it does not carry both meanings simultaneously. Language does not work that way, not in Hebrew nor in English. There is a lot of "great preaching" that makes poor biblical interpretation because of the violation this principle. See footnote 3 in chapter 5 for a caution.

The only exception to this iron-clad principle of interpretation is **when the author himself intends a double entendre**. In such a case the author is relying on the reader to know both ways he is using a word or expression. I don't know if Psalm 90:3 is an intentional double entendre, so the best counsel is caution.

Verse 3 is a statement of God executing the judgment of death He laid upon man in Genesis 3:19. There is some possible justification for seeing a secondary meaning in verse 3 as a call to repentance. The latter is tenuous and is better considered at present from a devotional, meditative standpoint than it is a technical, interpretative standpoint. Perhaps a genuine Hebrew scholar will comment at some point and settle the question decisively.

OUTLANDER CHRONICLES
BOOK ONE
PHOENIX

C.H. COBB

Survival and scavenging. Those are the two bywords for a world reeling from biological warfare. The future of humanity is in doubt when one young man decides that there must be more to life than mere survival. He encounters a mysterious mentor who buys in to his vision and the two collaborate to reestablish civilization. They might be successful—if they don't kill each other first.

Now available at chcobb.com and Amazon.com!

(Book 2 in this series is due out in 2015.)

A FALCON NOVEL

FALCON DOWN

C. H. COBB

Sometimes what you don't know really can hurt you . . .

While flying unarmed over international waters, Major Jacob "Falcon" Kelly's F-16 is downed by a Soviet missile. Captured after ejecting from his aircraft, Kelly is incarcerated in a secret interrogation center in Siberia, where he discovers the most daring and ruthless program of international espionage in the history of the Cold War. He faces torture, interrogation and certain death—unless he can escape. Escape seems impossible, but the Soviets' dossier on Kelly is missing two vital facts . . .

Now available at chcobb.com and Amazon.com!

A FALCON NOVEL

FALCON RISING

C. H. COBB

Major Jacob "Falcon" Kelly is a man without a country. The Russians want to kill him. The Americans think he's a traitor. Recently escaped from the USSR, yet facing arrest if he contacts American authorities, Kelly has no place to go. He knows that a KGB agent working undercover in the USAF will track his every move if he surfaces. Kelly possesses vital information that needs to find its way to the right people, but he doesn't know who to trust, or where to turn. Caught between Soviet assassins and the American intelligence services, Jake must run for his life!

Available in December, 2013, in time for Christmas!

About the Author

Chris Cobb's resume reads like a patchwork quilt. He's driven a forklift, worked as a technician doing component-level repair on digital circuitry, been a programmer-analyst, a data-center shift operator, taught high school science and mathematics, and been an Information Technology Director at a graduate school. Most of his career he's been a pastor.

He lives with his wife, Doris, in western Ohio, and is presently the teaching pastor at Bible Fellowship Church in Greenville, OH. They have three adult children, two fine sons-in-law and a wonderful daughter-in-law, all of whom are actively engaged serving Christ in the arts at some level.

Chris received Jesus Christ as his Savior in 1974, and seeks to incorporate a biblically faithful worldview into everything he does, including his writing.

You can find Chris on Facebook, or find additional works by him at chcobb.com.